Martin Jones

West Memphis Mojo

357 W 20th St., NY NY 10011
212 627-1055

WEST MEMPHIS MOJO

© Copyright 1986 by Martin Jones

All rights reserved. This work is fully protected under the copyright laws of the United States of America.

No part of this publication may be photocopied, reproduced, stored in a retrieval system, or transmitted, in any form or by any means, electronic, mechanical, recording, or otherwise, without the prior permission of the publisher. Additional copies of this play are available from the publisher.

Written permission is required for live performance of any sort. This includes readings, cuttings, scenes, and excerpts. For amateur and stock performances, please contact Broadway Play Publishing, Inc. For all other rights contact: Scott Hudson, 215 East 76th Street, New York, New York 10021.

First printing: April 1987
ISBN: 0-88145-049-9

Design by Marie Donovan
Front cover art by Anthony Russo
Set in Aster by L&F Technical Composition, Lakeland, FL
Printed on acid-free paper and bound by BookCrafters, Inc., Chelsea, MI

For Susan

West Memphis Mojo was a winner in the 1986 FDG/CBS New Plays Program. It premiered at the Northlight Theatre Company on March 19, 1986. Michael Maggio directed the following cast:

    TEDDY .... John Cothran, Jr.
    ELROI .... Don Franklin
    FRANK .... Gregory Alan-Williams
    MAXINE .... Lisa Dodson

    Song: "Can't Get Your Lovin' Off My Mind"—

        Music by Rick Snyder
        Lyrics by Martin Jones

The scenery was designed by Gary Baugh, the costumes by Kaye Nottbusch, and the lighting by Robert Shook. The Production Stage Manager was Anthony Berg.

West Memphis Mojo had its West Coast opening at the International City Theatre in Long Beach, California on January 16, 1987. Shashin Desai directed the following cast:

    TEDDY .... Jason Edwards
    ELROI .... Myles Thoroughgood
    FRANK .... Lee Hampton
    MAXINE .... Debra Thornton

Donald Gruber designed the set; Paulie Jenkins, the lighting; Michael A. Pacciorini, the costumes; Barbara Matthews, the make-up; and Mario Mariotta, the sound. Caryn Morse was the Assistant to the Director.

About the Author

Martin Jones was born in Elizabeth, New Jersey, but has lived primarily in the South and the Midwest, in places such as Memphis, St. Louis, Chicago, Michigan, Florida, and Virginia.

In 1968 he received a B.A. in English and Theatre Arts from Hillsdale College in Michigan. He received an M.A. in Theatre from Eastern Michigan University, and a Ph.D. in Playwriting and Dramatic Literature from Southern Illinois University in Carbondale, Illinois. While at Carbondale he studied creative writing with the novelist John Gardner.

For ten years Mr. Jones taught in academic theatre. He was Playwright-in-Residence at Northern Illinois University, and a drama professor at the University of Virginia and at Bowdoin College.

In 1980 he left academic theatre to work in Chicago as a playwright, actor, and director. He has worked as a performer at several regional theatres including the Victory Gardens Theatre, the Wisdom Bridge Theatre, the Theatre at Monmouth, and the Portland Stage Company.

In 1980 his play, *Old Soldiers*, premiered at the Performance Community in Chicago. *Old Soldiers* was published in *Best Short Plays of 1983*.

His play, *Daughters*, premiered at the Guthrie Theatre (Studio) in Minneapolis, and was later produced by Chicago's Victory Gardens Theatre. In 1982 two of his plays were staged Off-Off Broadway—*Flamingos*, at the Nameless Theatre, and *Snow Leopards*, at the 18th Street Playhouse. In October, 1983 his *Zoology* (a trilogy of plays) premiered in New York at the Stage Arts Theatre Company. In 1985 Stage Arts also produced *Snow Leopards*, which was published later that year by Samuel French.

West Memphis Mojo was selected in 1986 as a winner in the FDG/CBS New Plays Program. In the spring of that year, Mr. Jones co-authored a musical revue, *From Away*, which premiered at the Portland Stage Company.

Mr. Jones currently resides in Brunswick, Maine, and is the recipient of a Rockefeller Foundation Grant in Playwriting for 1986. He is currently Playwright-in-Residence at the Portland Stage Company.

Characters

Teddy (Early 40s) Black, owner and barber of Teddy's Barber Shop & Records in West Memphis, Arkansas.

Elroi (Late teens) Black, shoeshine boy in Teddy's shop. Fancies himself to be a songwriter.

Frank Jackson (Early 40s) Black, a blues singer and recording artist. Admired by Elroi.

Maxine Pettibone (Late 20s) White, housewife from Senatobia, Mississippi. Likes black musicians.

Time: A cold November in 1955.

Setting: Teddy's Barber Shop & Records in a poor black section of West Memphis, Arkansas.

ACT ONE

(*THE SET:* Consists of one main room: a barber shop with a record alcove.)

(*The shop is a storefront with a large bay window overlooking the street. The floor is worn linoleum, and the ceiling is made of painted tin, probably erected in the late 1920's. The walls are painted plaster and cheap wood paneling. There is a single barber chair of very old vintage, and a mirror, barber's sink, and shelves with clippers, razor, hair tonics on the wall behind the barber chair. A curtained doorway near the barber chair leads off to a back room. Against another wall is a shoeshine setup, with an elevated chair with brass footrests. At one corner of the shop there is an alcove with three small bins of phonograph records for sale. (In the South in the 50's, there were not many record stores, and as a result, most businesses in the black neighborhoods sold records as a sideline. People would purchase the latest R & B recordings in beauty parlors, drug stores, food markets, and barber shops.) Sitting next to the record bins is an old table-model record player, holding stacks of 78's, 45's, and few albums. Nearby, there is also an amplifier for an electric guitar, and an old flat-top, acoustic guitar with an electric pick-up installed in the sound hole of the guitar. The walls of the shop are adorned with the usual assortment of sepia pin-up girls, and there are several posters advertising Rhythm and Blues shows that have played at the Palace Theatre on Beale St., across the river in Memphis. Some of the posters are of Ike Turner's Kings of Rhythm Revue, B.B. King, Louis Jordan, and Joe Turner. On one section of wall there is a special section devoted to local deceased singing star, Johnny Ace—including a black and white autographed picture of the singer, a show poster, and the record cover of his major album—*"Johnny Ace—Memorial Album.")

(*MUSIC: Prior to the beginning of the play, Guitar Slim should be heard playing on the on-stage record player. As the lights dim to begin, his song, 'The Things That I Used To Do", can be heard.*)

(*AT RISE:* TEDDY, *a burly man in his early 40's, is seated in his barber chair, reading the Memphis World—the local black newspaper.* TEDDY *is dressed in dark slacks and an open-necked white shirt with a vest. He twiddles with his mustache and taps his foot along with the music as he reads. He turns and looks at himself in the mirror on the wall.* TEDDY *rises and moves closer to study his face in the reflection, as he hums along with the song. He takes some small barber's scissors from the shelf and trims his mustache. Finished, he smiles at himself. He goes to the window, looks out at the street, hands in pockets, rolling back and forth on the balls of his feet. The song ends.* TEDDY *goes to the record player and starts the record over again. He sits in the barber chair and resumes reading the paper. There is a knock at the front door of the shop.* TEDDY *tries to ignore it.*)

TEDDY: We're closed. It's Sunday.

(*Knocking continues.*)

TEDDY: You hear me? We closed. Who's out there?

ELROI: (*Outside*) Teddy. Open the door. It's me, Elroi.

TEDDY: (*Slowly rising.*) That you, Elroi?

ELROI: It's me. Open the goddamn door. Freezin' my ass off out here.

TEDDY: (*Opens door.*) Don't be cussin' out in the street. It's Sunday. Somebody's Mama be on her way to church . . . the whole neighborhood be on my butt.

(ELROI, *a young man in his late teens enters. He wears a light jacket and carries a brown paper sack with a*

Act One   3

change of clothes. Elroi *has a "do" rag on his head to protect his processed hairstyle.*)

Elroi: Ain't nobody on the street. Too damn cold. Brr.

Teddy: Where's your key?

Elroi: I gave it to Frank.

Teddy: He'll probably lose it. Close the door. You're lettin' all the heat outside.

Elroi: Damn it's cold. (*He closes the door, rubs his hands together, flaps his arms to warm up.*)

Teddy: You get my licorice?

Elroi: (*Tosses him a sack.*) Yeah, I got it . . . had to go three places . . . find somethin' open.

Teddy: (*Savoring a piece*) Thanks. Well, don't stand there flappin' your arms. Get over here, stand on the hot air vent.

(Elroi *stands over the heating vent.*)

Elroi: Coldest damn winter I ever seen. Radio says it gonna snow.

Teddy: It ain't gonna snow. It's only November.

Elroi: Said it on WDIA . . .

Teddy: Ain't never snowed in November . . .

Elroi: All I know . . . it's cold in Tennessee!!

(Elroi *elongates the word "Tennessee".*)

Teddy: Why you always say that?

Elroi: What?

Teddy: (*Mimics* Elroi) "Tennessee!" We's in Arkansas, fool! Cross the river, or has you got chillbrains too? (Teddy *laughs at his own joke.*) "Cold in Tennessee". You got that from Frank . . . that's where you got that from. I heard him say it too.

ELROI: Yeah. He says it sometimes.

TEDDY: Where'd he get it?

ELROI: Dunno. Have to ask him yourself. Somethin' he heard . . . I guess.

TEDDY: You want some coffee? I got water on in the back room. You want . . . I get you a cup . . .

ELROI: That be great. With lotsa sugar . . .

(TEDDY *goes off through a curtained area that leads to a back room—his living quarters in the back of the shop.* ELROI *hangs up his jacket on a hook on the wall. He picks up* TEDDY'S *copy of the paper, sits in the barber chair.*)

ELROI: Anything in the paper?

TEDDY: (*Off, teasing*) What do you care? You can't read.

ELROI: Hell, I can't.

TEDDY: (*Off*) Guitar Slim's playin' at the Pearl Lounge next week.

ELROI: (*Scanning the paper.*) I know, Frank told me. Hey, there be somethin' 'bout Big Boy Crudup . . .

(TEDDY *enters carrying* ELROI'S *coffee, and a cup for himself.*)

TEDDY: Where? Lemme see that.

ELROI: No, man. I found it. I get to read it first.

(*They struggle over the paper.*)

TEDDY: Now, give me my paper. C'mon give it up . . .

ELROI: (*Holding it away from* TEDDY.) You had it all mornin'. I want a chance. I been out runnin' your errands. I should get to see the *World*.

TEDDY: You gonna be seein' stars in about one second. Gimme my paper.

Act One   5

(*To keep it from* TEDDY, ELROI *sits on the newspaper.*)

ELROI: You want it? You reach your hand under my butt for it. Come on. (*Laughs*) I been workin' up a big ol' fart for when you do.

TEDDY: All right, fool! Take the paper. But, first... you get outta my chair. You can read it to me... you need the practice. Begin with the story about Big Boy Crudup.

(ELROI *rises, moves to the shoeshine chair.* TEDDY *sits in the barber chair.*)

ELROI: It says here that Mr. Elvis Presley has made Arthur Big Boy Crudup a famous man, by recordin' one of his songs... "That's All Right, Mama"... (*Pause*) What about "Milk Cow Blues?"

TEDDY: Just read the article.

ELROI: (*Reading*) "Crudup was not even aware that his song had been recorded until he heard Presley's version of "That's All Right, Mama," on a radio broadcast from WLAC in Nashville..."

TEDDY: John R's show, I bet. "Brought to you by Randy's Record Mart in Gallatin, Tennessee..."

ELROI: You wanna hear the article or not?

TEDDY: Go on.

ELROI: (*Reading*) "Arthur Crudup, or Big Boy, as his friends call him, is not currently active in the recording industry. He was known for many recordings on various "race record" labels made during the 1940's. Crudup now lives on a sharecropper farm near Greenwood, Mississippi. He says that he is rather bewildered by all the attention that Mr. Presley has brought to him. But, as he says, "I'll be glad if they send me some money."

TEDDY: Yeah, I bet. Big Boy Crudup got enough socked away to buy him a whole fleet of Cadillacs. Can't tell me he's choppin' cotton in Mississippi, not a big star like that. Naw, I bet he just says that so every freeloadin' nigger in the Delta don't come hittin' on him for a handout.

ELROI: You think so?

TEDDY: Sure. Crudup ain't nobody's fool. Before the war ... I seen him once ... at the Palace over on Beale ... him and Louis Jordan. Hell of a show. Limousines all lined up at the curb ... women in fur coats ... nothin' like it. They was popular with white folks too. Had to do two different shows every night—one early for the whites, and one later for the coloreds. Standin' room only a whole week runnin'. Them singers get rich, boy, and that's a fact. (*Pause*) So, read me the rest of it.

ELROI: That's all it says.

TEDDY: That's all?

ELROI: Ain't nothin', but about two inches in here.

TEDDY: Hmmm. Ain't that somethin'?

(*They are quiet.* ELROI *turns on the radio. Gospel music is heard coming from the radio.* TEDDY *looks at the radio.*)

TEDDY: What the hell is that on my radio?

ELROI: Sounds like Rosie Wallace.

TEDDY: (*Rises*) I hate Gospel music. Screamin' 'bout Jesus ... makes me jumpy. (*Turns off radio.*) Got no sophistication. Ain't got no uptown rhythm. You know what I mean?

ELROI: Oh yeah. Not like what we can do.

TEDDY: (*Crossing to window*) Not hardly. (*Looks at street.*) Terrible lookin' day ... even for a Sunday. (*Pause*) What time did Frank say he was gonna get here?

ELROI: About noon, I guess. The session is at two. Why? You nervous?

TEDDY: Me, nervous? Naw. What do we do if he don't come by here first? Suppose he goes right over to Memphis?

ELROI: He ain't goin' nowheres without his amplifier and guitar...

(TEDDY *looks skeptically at the guitar.*)

TEDDY: So, where the hell is he?

ELROI: You is nervous.

TEDDY: No... I just need me a taste, that's all. (*Looks out window.*) Goddamn Blue laws. I wish I had me some corn liquor.

(ELROI *chuckles gleefully, rises, and goes to his sack of clothing on the floor near the coat rack.* ELROI *pulls out a fifth of Heaven Hill bourbon, holds it proudly.*)

ELROI: Suppose I said I have a surprise for you? Somethin' better than a twenty-five cent slab of corn ... look here.

TEDDY: Where the hell'd you get that on a Sunday? You bust in a liquor store?

ELROI: No, Teddy. This is somethin' I been savin'... for a special occasion... Heaven Hill. What do you think about that?

TEDDY: You done stole it off a truck somewhere.

ELROI: What do you care where I got it? Give me your cup. We give you a taste right now. Come on. (*He opens the bottle.*)

TEDDY: I know where you got that... one of them bootleggers on President's Island. Probably been watered... cut with tea.

ELROI: No, sir. Genuine... bottled in bond. Ain't no bootlegger's keep. Stuff is smooth... goes down like honey-dew rind water. You gonna like this. (ELROI *pours them both a cup of bourbon.*) Try that on.

(TEDDY *drinks slowly, savoring the whiskey.*)

TEDDY: Mighty fine. I know you stole this shit. Pour me another.

ELROI: Take it slow. We gotta be sharp today.

TEDDY: I'm always sharp, boy. Wherever you got this bourbon . . . I hope you had the good sense to walk off with a couple of dozen cases . . .

ELROI: Naw, I only got two bottles. A waiter over at the Peabody Hotel sneaked 'em out after work. Pretty good, huh? I figured that since you and me is about to get ourselves famous like Big Boy Crudup . . . I thought we should celebrate with the good stuff.

TEDDY: Yeah, could be our lucky day . . . (*He pours himself another drink.*) You better watch Frank around that bottle. He'll drink it all . . .

ELROI: Be our secret.

TEDDY: So where do you think he is? Probably some gin mill!

ELROI: Maybe he got a woman shacked up in Memphis.

TEDDY: Better get his butt over here . . . after twelve now . . .

ELROI: Why don't you just sit and relax, Teddy. He'll be here.

TEDDY: What if he comes in drunk? And he can't sing?

ELROI: Then we sober him up.

TEDDY: What if he's in jail?

ELROI: Then we get ourselves another singer.

ACT ONE

TEDDY: Like who?

ELROI: You and me.

(TEDDY *guffaws*)

ELROI: Why not? We can sing 'em. We wrote 'em, so we can sing 'em too. (*Sings*)

She got a mean disposition
She's the meanest gal I ever seen
I asked her for some whiskey
And all I got was kerosene
Hey, darlin', why you gotta be so mean?

Take it, Teddy ... Dee, dee, da, dum ...

TEDDY: Dee, dee my ass ... I ain't no singer. And I don't play that damn guitar.

ELROI: Me, neither. (*Pause*) All right, so we need Frank. Aw, don't get riled up. Frank ain't no fool. This is his big chance too. He knows Sun Records ain't gonna come lookin' for him ... that's why I know, he's gonna show up. You gotta have some faith, Teddy. You turnin' white.

TEDDY: (*Pouring a drink.*) I don't know why I let you talk me into this. All your big ideal ... writin' rhythm and blues songs ... nobody ever heard of us.

ELROI: But they done heard of Frank. And soon, they gonna hear of us. We all be rich men. (*Laughs*) Can I use the back room for a minute?

TEDDY: What for?

ELROI: I wanna change my clothes. Gotta look sharp when we get over to Memphis.

TEDDY: Go ahead.

(ELROI *picks up his sack of clothes, looks at* TEDDY.)

ELROI: You goin' like that?

TEDDY: What's wrong with this? It's clean shirt.

ELROI: You might wanna wear a tie. We just might be talkin' to white folks.

TEDDY: I got nothin' to say to them white folks.

ELROI: Then, you keep quiet. Me and Frank will do the talkin'.

TEDDY: You pretty sure of yourself, ain't you?

ELROI: (*Exits to back room.*) Why not? What we got to lose?

(*Offstage,* ELROI *sings* "Can't Get Your Lovin' Off My Mind"—*see lyrics at end of play.* TEDDY *looks at himself in the mirror. He opens a drawer and finds a bow tie. He puts on the tie, looks at himself, feels foolish, loses his nerve, and removes the tie.*)

TEDDY: Oh, what am I doin'? Who am I foolin'? I ain't no songwriter. I'm a barber . . . that's all.

ELROI: (*Off*) Seems I recall you sayin' somethin' different, last time you heard Frank rehearsin', "Can't Get Your Lovin' Off My Mind."

TEDDY: Yeah . . . (*Pause*) Did sound pretty good, didn't it?

ELROI: (*Off*) Better song than, "That's All Right, Mama."

TEDDY: That be true! But, then Big Boy Crudup had that Presley kid to help out.

ELROI: (*Off*) You'll see . . . gonna be the same for us. We get some white guy to sing the songs . . . we be right up there. We gonna make it, Teddy. You just gotta keep tellin' yourself that the three of us come up with somethin' that's good. Gonna change our lives!

(ELROI *enters wearing orange pants, a dark silk shirt, and a white tie. He struts in front of the mirror. He still has the handkerchief tied over his head.*)

ACT ONE

TEDDY: You gonna wear the rag on your head too?

(ELROI *removes the handkerchief from his processed hair. He primps in the mirror.*)

ELROI: This here, keeps the rain offa my "do" ... keeps it just perfect.

(ELROI *primps his head in the mirror. He dabs a place with one of the handtowels.*)

TEDDY: Hey, don't be gummin' up my clean barber towels with that process junk. I'll never get them towels clean.

ELROI: My hair is clean.

TEDDY: Can't believe you'd put that junk on your hair ...

ELROI: Man, it's in style.

TEDDY: Gonna make all your hair fall out, you'll be bald-headed.

ELROI: Not my hair.

TEDDY: What do you think they put in that stuff, huh? It's lye ... that stuff is poison, boy ... you can kill varmints with it. I ain't lyin' to ya. ... I'm a barber ... I know somethin' about hair. Stuff will kill your scalp. (*Long pause*) Okay so don't listen to me. You'll see what I'm talkin' about.

ELROI: You just tryin' to scare me. Probably ain't even true. You just sayin' that cause you ain't got a "do" like mine. You jealous ... that's what.

TEDDY: That'll be the day.

ELROI: You gonna be a wooly head 'til the day you die.

TEDDY: Coloreds ain't meant to have straight hair. Ain't natural.

ELROI: (*Points to photo on wall.*) What about Johnny Ace? Look at his picture! You can't tell me that's natural. That hair done been played with.

TEDDY: Johnny mighta put a hot comb through it once, or twice, but he wasn't no conk head ... Look like some Eye-talian!

(ELROI *douses himself with some Lilac aftershave.*)

TEDDY: Go easy on that Lilac Vegetal. Got to last me 'til the end of the month.

ELROI: Now I smell pretty.

TEDDY: Won't have to take no bath 'til Christmas, right? Fool! Usin' up all my inventory!

ELROI: (*In mirror*) I be lookin' bad, just like Chuck Berry. (*Sings*)

"Mabellene why can't you be true?
You done started back doin'
The things you used to do.
Maybellene..."

(ELROI *does the* "Chuck Berry Duck Walk.")

ELROI: (*Strikes a pose*) So, what do you think? Has you ever seen anything look so good in your entire life?

(TEDDY *regards the image for a moment, breaks into a wide smile, and then laughs hysterically.*)

TEDDY: Lawd, have mercy!

ELROI: What's wrong? Why you laughin'? What's so funny?

TEDDY: (*Pointing at the pants.*) You be Orangebird! With them skinny legs, and all....

ELROI: Knock it off. You and Frank been callin' me that Orangebird.... and I'm sick of it...

TEDDY: (*Laughing*) An Orangebird ... that's what you is ...

ELROI: Don't start that shit, again. My name is Elroi ... I don't like that other name...

TEDDY: Well, look at yourself in the mirror, fool! You ridiculous! Am I right? Ol' Crazy-legs Orangebird!

ELROI: That ain't my name! Now, cut that shit, Teddy. I don't like it.

TEDDY: Everytime you wear them pants, I'm gonna call you Orangebird.

ELROI: How you like it if I call you fat nappyhead?

TEDDY: (*After a pause*) You'd be lookin' to swallow some teeth.

ELROI: Then, you lay off, man! My name is Elroi. E-L-R-O-I. My Mama said my name means, The King ... in French. You know that? You wanna call me somethin' else ... you call me, The King! That's what!

TEDDY: You lucky your Mama ain't alive to see the mess she raised.

ELROI: Okay. You wanna talk about your Mama ... we talk about your Mama ...

TEDDY: Hey! Don't be startin' no dozens with me, boy! I don't allow that ... not in here! I mean it! I don't tolerate the dozens ... not outta your mouth! Where's your respect?

(*Silence.* ELROI *moves away, sullen.*)

TEDDY: You hear me?

ELROI: I hear ya. Then, you lay offa that Orangebird crap!

TEDDY: All right ... I'll do that.

ELROI: I can't help it. I got skinny legs. I had rickets when I was a kid. Ain't my fault.

TEDDY: I know. All right, I'm sorry ... shouldn't have started that ...

ELROI: I spent ten dollars on these pants . . . and I like 'em. They sharp. I only got two pairs of pants . . . these, and them ol' black ones.

TEDDY: I said I was sorry, Elroi. . . . let's just drop it, okay?

ELROI: Okay.

TEDDY: Let's have us a drink. "C'mon." (TEDDY *pours the drinks.*) To us . . . and to The King!

ELROI: That's right, The King! . . . El-Roi! And to Nappyhead Teddy . . . and to Guitar Frank Jackson, our partner!

(TEDDY *downs his drink*)

TEDDY: I'm gonna call that guitar playin' low life . . .

(TEDDY *gets a coin from his change drawer, goes to the pay phone on a wall near the door. He finds a piece of paper in his vest pocket with the number.* TEDDY *dials the number, after dropping in the coin.*)

TEDDY: (*To* ELROI) If he's still sleepin', then it's time to be gettin' up. It's ringin' . . . (*To phone*) Who's this? Is this the King Cotton Hotel? Get me Frank Jackson's room, please. Jackson, like Stonewall! That's right . . . tell him it's an emergency. What? When? Son of a bitch! No . . . that's okay. Did he say where he was goin'? Well . . . is he comin' back? I see. Well . . . if he does, you tell him to call TEDDY over in West Memphis. It's real important. 'Bye. (TEDDY *hangs up.*)

ELROI: He ain't there?

TEDDY: He done checked out of the King Cotton last night.

ELROI: Last night. What the hell for?

TEDDY: I dunno. The man at the desk don't know nothin'. Frank jes up and left in the night . . . took all his shit outta the room.

ELROI: Maybe he's plannin' to move it over here . . .

TEDDY: What for?

ELROI: I dunno . . . just an idea.

TEDDY: I don't like it. Maybe we oughta call the recordin' studio . . . in Memphis . . . that Sun Records. You got the number?

ELROI: There ain't no point in callin'. It's Sunday. They gonna be closed.

TEDDY: How can they be closed? We gotta recordin' session at two!

ELROI: Front office gonna be closed. Only the engineer be there to meet us this afternoon.

TEDDY: What are you sayin'?

ELROI: We're goin' in kinda on the sly. The only reason we gettin' in to record is 'cause Frank knows this engineer guy . . . and there ain't nobody usin' the studio on Sunday. See, Frank got it set up so we get in, cut our songs, and get gone 'fore anybody knows nothin'. Then, sometime next week, or two . . . the recordin' engineer . . . he take our record in to Sam Phillips . . . say, "Hey, I found this. . . . Listen to these guys. . . . This is some great shit." So, Sam Phillips, he listens to the songs, he digs it, and he flip out, sayin' he gotta give us a big contract right away . . . and there you are! We be set . . . we on our way!

TEDDY: Why we gotta sneak in the back door?

ELROI: 'Cause that's the way it works. Frank says we go in the front we get thrown out on our ass. These cats at Sun, they got Elvis Presley. . . . They big time now. You think they gonna give a damn about three coloreds from nowhere 'cross the river? No way.

TEDDY: They gonna change their tune when they hear them songs we wrote!

ELROI: Of course . . . but, we got to go 'bout it the right way. Frank says it's the best shot . . . go through the engineer.

TEDDY: I don't know . . . I'm gonna call the studio, jes' see if he's over there.

ELROI: Don't do it, Teddy. What if there's somebody in the office . . . like one of those white guys . . . and you get the wrong guy on the line . . . ?

TEDDY: So. I ask to speak to the egineer. What's his name?

ELROI: I dunno. Frank didn't tell me.

TEDDY: So . . . how many colored engineers they gonna have?

ELROI: That's not cool. What you gonna say? "Hello, can I speak to the nigger in the booth?" You do that, it be fucked and we out for good. No record. Give him some time. Shit, it ain't but half past now . . . I know Frank . . . he ain't gonna cut an' run . . . I say we sit tight . . . wait a spell.

TEDDY: Okay, okay . . . maybe you right. (*Pause*) Son of a bitch, got forty dollars of mine!

ELROI: What?

TEDDY: Said he had to get his red guitar out of hock.

ELROI: What red guitar?

TEDDY: You tell me.

ELROI: What's the matter with this here guitar?

TEDDY: That's what I asked him. He said that ol' flat top model ain't got the right tone. He says he got an electric one on ice with one of them Jew stores on Beale street . . . said he need forty dollars to get it out. I tried to call him on it, he said to talk to you 'bout it . . . said you'd know what guitar he was talkin' about.

ELROI: Ain't never seen Frank play no red 'lectric guitar.

TEDDY: Me neither. Didn't know he owned one. (*Looks at guitar.*) This one sounded fine to me. He played on it all last month. Nothin' wrong with the tone . . . not in my ear . . . (*Pause, then a recognition.*) He done stole my money to get hisself a new guitar! That's what that lyin' mutha done . . .

ELROI: Wait a minute . . . don't go flyin' off. We don't know what's what!

TEDDY: I been suckered! That's what! Cheat me out of my money . . . Well, I tell you that forty dollars is comin' out of his cut . . . ain't comin' out of mine!

ELROI: Okay. We work it out when he gets here. Calm down, Teddy. You gonna get your blood pressure up.

TEDDY: That no-count done piss me off! Never shoulda listened to his stories . . . and yours too! . . . let you drag my butt into this foolishness . . .

ELROI: You gotta relax. Teddy. Frank ain't gonna pull a fast one on you.

TEDDY: You ain't known him as long as I have. He's just a no-count drifter, that's what he is. You's a fool to believe anything he says. I know him boy, he ain't nobody's angel.

ELROI: (*Massaging* TEDDY) Hey! Hey! Cool out, Teddy. You're gonna have a stroke or somethin'. We gonna cut our songs today. So, you just save it. Look at you . . . your're sweatin', breathin' hard, your knees are twitchin' . . .

TEDDY: Then quit shakin' me, boy!

ELROI: Maybe you need one of your pills.

TEDDY: They on the dresser in the back room.

(ELROI *goes off.* TEDDY *wipes his face, fans himself with the newpaper, and breathes heavily.* ELROI *re-enters with a pill bottle of blood pressure medicine.*

He goes to the sink, finds a glass, fills it with water, and gives both to TEDDY.)

ELROI: You gonna be okay?

TEDDY: Yeah. I be all right.

ELROI: You don't look so hot. You want me to get the chiropractor?

TEDDY: No, I be all right. Jes, let me sit a spell . . . get my wind.

ELROI: Can't have you dyin' on me, Teddy. Not today.

TEDDY: (*Fanning with paper*) I made it through the war . . . I'll make it through this day. Don't worry 'bout me. Look out for yourself. Christ, it's hot in here. Crack that front door.

ELROI: You'll get a chill.

TEDDY: Open the door, Elroi!

(ELROI *opens the door slightly*.)

TEDDY: And while you're at it, pour me another Heaven Hill.

ELROI: That be a sure way to get to Heaven.

TEDDY: You gonna sass me? Do what I say. I know what I'm doin'.

(ELROI *pours another drink in* TEDDY'S *glass*.)

TEDDY: Get yourself one, too.

ELROI: Seein' how it's my bourbon . . . you know, you worry me.

TEDDY: I been livin' with high blood all my life, boy. I'll be fine . . . soon as these pills kick in.

ELROI: How'd they ever let you in the service? Woulda thought they'd make you 4-F, or somethin'.

TEDDY: Hell . . . time I went in . . . 1943 . . . they woulda taken anybody . . . even a cripple. They was desperate.

ACT ONE   19

They didn't put me in the fightin' troops. Put me in
the Quartermaster Corps. Did my time at a base in
England. They made me a barber . . . heard my Daddy
cut hair, guess they figured I cut hair, too. But, I ain't
complainin' . . . Army was good to me. Didn't get my
ass shot up by no Nazis. I did okay. After D-Day, in
'44, most of the regular troops was over on the Conti-
nent . . . that's what they call Europe . . . the Conti-
nent! Anyway, there wasn't too many haircuts to be
givin' for about eight months. So, I fixed it so I spent
most of my time on leave. In London. Nice city, London. Met me some pretty girls.

ELROI: I bet they got some pretty gals over there.

TEDDY: Sure they do . . . white, Chinese, African, Jamai-
cans, Hindu . . . Siameses . . . they got 'em in all colors
over there, boy! A veritable rainbow! They look so fine,
look like God done thrown down some angels out of
heaven.

ELROI: Sounds like the place for me.

TEDDY: Yeah, I liked it over there in London . . . seemed
like paradise, you know? First place I ever been
where folks didn't treat ya like you was some ol' dog.
See, it's different over there . . . color don't seem to
keep folks apart like it does back home. You see men
like Duke Ellington, and Louis Armstrong—they're
treated like kings over there. I seen a picture in the
paper . . . Duke Ellington kissing the hand of the
Queen of England! Imagine that! Kissin' her hand . . .
and it's on the front page of the paper! Try that over
in Memphis . . . they'd nail your carcass to the
bridge, 'til the buzzards picked you clean. (*Pause*)
Yeah . . . England . . . spent the finest eight months
of my life there. (*Reminiscing*) I had me a nice little
Irish girl for a while, name of Marie . . . coal black
hair, blue eyes . . . skin like alabaster. I coulda mar-
ried that girl if I'd wanted to . . . her family didn't
mind . . . and she was Catholic. But I didn't care
about that, you know? (TEDDY *broods into his drink*)

Sometimes I wonder what it would have been like if I'd just stayed on over there after the war . . . lot of our boys did, you know?

ELROI: Why'd you come back? I woulda stayed . . .

TEDDY: I had responsibilities back here in West Memphis . . . when my father took sick . . . wasn't nobody to run the shop (*Pause*) maybe I'll take you over there sometime . . .

ELROI: Yeah . . . just as soon as we get Elvis Presley to sing our songs. Yes, sir . . . I be out of here for good. London, here we come!

TEDDY: Last week we was goin' to Chicago. Week before that, it was where? Harlem?

ELROI: Hell, I go anyplace outta the South. Someplace where I don't have to keep my eyes down just cause there's somebody white in the room.

TEDDY: You dreamin' . . . 'taint never gonna be that way in this country.

ELROI: Unless you a big star . . . like Johnny Ace! He didn't have to take crap from nobody . . . white, or colored.

TEDDY: Johanny was different . . . the exception. Not many like him.

ELROI: First time I heard him sing, I knew that's what I wanted. Just like that. Everbody know my name . . . walk down the sidewalk with a gal on each arm . . . stroll right on up to the front door of the Peabody Hotel, walk right past the doorman, on up to the register desk . . . get me a suite of rooms . . . with champagne to boot! Jes, like that!

TEDDY: Even Johnny Ace never got in the front door of the Peabody Hotel.

ELROI: Someday . . . it gonna happen.

TEDDY: Not in my lifetime.

ACT ONE

ELROI: Maybe I be the one . . .

TEDDY: You drunk with glory, boy.

(TEDDY *goes over to the record player and plays the second side of the Johnny Ace single. The song "Never Let Me Go" begins.*)

ELROI: (*Recognizing the tune*) My man . . . Johnny.

TEDDY: Best of the uptown singers.

(TEDDY *leans back closes his eyes, and listens to the plaintive tone of Johnny Ace's singing.*)

ELROI: (*Nostalgic*) Man, he could sing . . .

TEDDY: The best of the best . . .

ELROI: Why did the fool wanna kill hisself? He had it all . . . money, women, sharp cars . . . everything. (*Pause*) I remember the night I heard he was dead . . . last year . . . what was it? . . . New Year's Eve . . .

TEDDY: (*Correcting*) Christmas Eve.

ELROI: Right, Christmas Eve.

TEDDY: (*Reclining, with eyes closed*) Backstage at the City Auditorium, Houston, Texas . . . intermission of the Christmas show . . . Johnny put a bullet in the chamber of his pistol, spun it around, put the gun to his head, and pulled the trigger. (*Pause*) Never finished the show.

ELROI: What a waste. Playin' Russian Roulette . . . You knew the guy . . . why he wanta do somethin' crazy like that?

TEDDY: I dunno . . . folks said he did it to impress some girl . . .

ELROI: White girl, I bet.

TEDDY: Pink Miller says it wasn't no accident . . . he was just bored . . . bored with livin'. I remember him from the ol' days in Memphis . . . he always liked to play cards ... and he carried a pistol, even back then ... always pullin' it out, twirlin' it around ... cockin' that piece, like he was crazy or somethin.

You shoulda seen him the last time he played the Palace in Memphis.... The whole crowd was real impatient during the opening act ... Big Mama Thornton, had to get off early.... Then Johnny come out and all hell broke loose. He had all the girls up close, crowdin' the edge of the stage, and on them ballads he'd lean over to 'em ... real close and sexy, like he was singin' just to them. Girls would start screamin' like a snake bit 'em.

ELROI: Man, I wish I'd been there.

TEDDY: Couldn't half hear the music ... bitches swoonin' in the aisles. (*Laughs*) Women was always chasin' after Johnny Alexander ... that was his real name, back when he went to Washinton High School.

ELROI: How'd you meet him?

TEDDY: I met him after he come back from the Navy. Every Friday night, Frank, and me, and Johnny, Pink Miller, and some other guys ... we used to play cards over in the back room of Dinky's Tavern ... offa Lamar Boulevard. Them was some nights, I tell you. And Johnny ... he was always showin' off that pistol ... (*Long pause*) Them days is gone now. (*Pause*) I went to the funeral. Everybody in Memphis ... seems like was there ... never seen so many flowers. And the fans ... shit, girls was weepin' and moanin' ... tryin' to throw themselves on top the casket. Police had to come ... pry 'em off ... just to get the coffin in the ground.

(*The record ends.* ELROI *goes to the record player.*)

ELROI: You wanna hear the other side?

TEDDY: Yeah, that be fine. But, keep your greasy fingers offa the record surface. I can't sell those things to folks if they got your finger prints all over them.

ELROI: You ain't gonna sell this record, been played so many times, the grooves 'bout done wore out.

(ELROI *puts record on.* "Pledging My Love," *Johnny Ace's most famous song.* ELROI *mimes a singing routine in the mirror.* ELROI *gets an idea for a song. he turns off the record, finds a pencil, tears off part of paper bag to write on.*)

ELROI: Teddy, we gotta write us a ballad like that. Now, help me out . . .

(ELROI *sits near* TEDDY. ELROI *hums a tune similar to a Johnny Ace ballad tempo.* ELROI *struggles to find the first line of the song.*)

ELROI: (*Sings as he scribbles.*)

Don't leave me my darlin'
Why won't you be true?

(TEDDY *watches, helpless to add any idea to the process.*)

ELROI: Come on, Teddy . . . help me out . . .

TEDDY: I'm thinkin' Elroi . . . I'm thinkin' . . .

ELROI: (*Sings and scribbles.*) I always think of you . . .

TEDDY: (*Following* ELROI's *lead.*) . . . always think of you . . .

ELROI: (*Starts over—singing.*)

Don't leave me my darlin'
Why don't you be true?

(TEDDY *joins in, unsure*)

I always think of you. . . .
Don't make me feel . . . . .

(*Pause*)

TEDDY: (*Blurts out gleefully.*) BLUE! Blue . . . that's it . . .

ELROI: (*Singing and scribbling.*)

I always think of you
Don't make me feel blue . . .

ELROI: (*Turns the paper over to begin anew.*) All right, that's the first verse . . . now the second one. Come on . . . help me here, Teddy. You listenin' to me? Talk to me . . .

TEDDY: (*After a pause*) We dreamin' . . . that's all we doin'.

ELROI: (*Throws pencil down.*) You gettin' in a funk on me again?

TEDDY: We ain't got no experience as songwriters. Who we kiddin'? I can't come up with songs like that, Elroi. Not a chance.

ELROI: Hey, where's your confidence?

TEDDY: Done been kicked outta me. I ain't as young as you, Elroi. I been around. I seen what's possible . . . and what ain't . . .

ELROI: Man, what is wrong with you? We got talent.

TEDDY: Just foolin' ourselves . . .

ELROI: You got a bad attitude, Teddy. You gettin' sad-eyed drunk on me, and you not makin' sense . . . just feelin' sorry for yourself. We gonna make it with a charm . . . see, we got a special kind of luck on our side. I wanna show you somethin . . .

(ELROI *goes to his jacket hanging on a hook. From the pocket, he pulls out a "mojo hand"—a talisman, wrapped in red flannel with a dark string attached.* ELROI *shows the mojo to* TEDDY.)

ELROI: Look here . . . we got magic with us.

TEDDY: What is that thing?

ELROI: It's a mojo.

ACT ONE

TEDDY: Aw, for Chrissake!

ELROI: I was gonna give it to Frank . . . but, I reckon you need it worse than him . . . it be a charm, see . . .

TEDDY: Get that thing away from me.

ELROI: C'mon, I went to the conjure woman, and she made it up special for us.

TEDDY: Ol' conjure woman is nothin' but a fake.

ELROI: She is not.

TEDDY: How can you believe in that voodoo?

ELROI: Ain't voodoo. It's powerful medicine. I know, 'cause my Mama went to the conjure woman when I was bad sick . . . conjure woman made up one of her spells . . . put a mojo on my body . . . and them rickets, just cleared up. It's the truth . . . done went away. I could walk normal again . . . Doctors said I might never get outta the bed . . . and the conjure woman, she cured me.

TEDDY: You's a fool to believe that.

ELROI: It's good magic. She done fixed it up, and it's guaranteed. She say it bring back a lost love, give a person good luck . . . can even chase out the devil.

TEDDY: Them things is curses too.

ELROI: Not this one. I told her . . . we be needin' good fortune. Now, you put this on . . . you see if it don't change your whole outlook . . . maybe even lower your blood pressure, too.

TEDDY: I ain't gonna wear nothin' made by that ol' witch.

ELROI: C'mon, it ain't gonna bite you. Try it on.

TEDDY: (*Moves away*) Conjure woman is the ugliest lookin' woman on God's Earth. Face like a monkey . . . scrawny legs . . . look like a twisted 'possum . . .

ELROI: You scared of the mojo, ain't you? You scared it might have the power . . . ain't that right?

TEDDY: I ain't scared of that little sack.

ELROI: Then why won't you touch it?

TEDDY: Damn foolishness.

ELROI: Touch the mojo.

TEDDY: It's a sin against the Lord.

ELROI: Since when you go to church?

TEDDY: It ain't right.

ELROI: Look at you. You is scared.

TEDDY: No I ain't.

ELROI: Okay, then . . . put out your hand. Take the mojo . . . jes hold it in your hand. It ain't gonna hurt you.

(*Reluctantly,* TEDDY *takes the sack.*)

TEDDY: What she put in here?

ELROI: Potions.

TEDDY: (*Sniffs the mojo.*) Smells like somethin' rotten.

ELROI: Means it's doin' its work.

TEDDY: What's in this thing . . . make it smell so bad?

ELROI: I don't know what all . . . some herbs . . . Samson's snakeroot, Devil's shoestring, some flour, a lump of coal . . . drippings . . . I don't know everything . . . but it works. She said some words over it, and it give off smoke. I swear . . . I seen the smoke.

TEDDY: (*Tries to hand it to* ELROI.) Here . . . take it back.

ELROI: Say your full name.

TEDDY: What?

ELROI: Just say your full name. Come on . . . say it . . .

TEDDY: What for?

ELROI: Just do it. Full name . . . not just Teddy.

TEDDY: Theodore Booker Nalls. Satisfied? Now, take this stupid thing back.

ELROI: I can't.

TEDDY: Why not?

ELROI: It's yours now. The spell be workin'. See, you done said your name over it . . . it belongs to you . . . won't work for nobody but the name it hears last.

TEDDY: Well, I don't want it.

ELROI: Too late now. You got it.

TEDDY: I ain't wearin' this thing!

ELROI: You got to. Put it 'round your neck.

TEDDY: What if I say your name over it?

ELROI: Won't work right. I'd have to be holdin' it, and I'd have to say it . . . besides, a mojo ain't supposed to change hands, once they been adopted . . . be like throwin' out a child . . . maybe bring on a curse.

TEDDY: Are you shittin' me?

ELROI: No, that's what the conjure woman say, and she don't lie. The mojo is yours . . . better put it 'round your neck.

TEDDY: What happens if I don't?

ELROI: I dunno. I ain't sure I wanna find out.

(TEDDY *looks at the mojo, and finally slips the string over his head.*)

TEDDY: Are you happy now? Do I have to wear it all the time? Even when I'm sleeping?

ELROI: Don't know... I'll have to ask the woman... you best keep it on 'til we find out what to do next.

(TEDDY *tries to hide the mojo, placing it inside his shirt.*)

TEDDY: People see this thing... they think I'm nuts. (*Pulls out the mojo from inside his shirt.*) Damn thing itches. You talk to her first thing tomorrow, 'cause ain't no way I'm gonna wear this thing all the time.

ELROI: I'll ask her. So... how you feelin'?

TEDDY: I feel like an idiot.

ELROI: You know... different? Relaxed?... what do you feel?

TEDDY: Nothin! Was you expectin' smoke?

ELROI: Maybe we done it wrong... left somethin' out...

TEDDY: If I get poisoned, or I die from this thing... you gonna be in some big trouble...

(*Pay phone rings. They stare at it for a moment. It rings again.*)

ELROI: Frank! It's Frank... see, the charm is workin'.

TEDDY: I'll get it. (*Answers phone.*) Hello... who? This is him... speakin'.

ELROI: Is it him?

(TEDDY *nods.*)

Where is he? Is he comin'?

(TEDDY *shoos him away.*)

TEDDY: Operator, where is this call coming from?

ELROI: Long distance?

TEDDY: (*On phone*) Helena? You mean Helena, Arkansas?

ELROI: What the fuck he doin' in Helena?

ACT ONE 29

TEDDY: (*To phone*) Yes, ma'm... I'm sorry,... I didn't mean to cuss in your ear...

ELROI: Don't he know we gotta make a record in an hour?

TEDDY: (*To phone*) 'Scuse me a minute, ma'am.

ELROI: He supposed to be here...

TEDDY: (*Covers receiver, to* ELROI.) Stop your jabberin'... and just maybe I can find out what's goin' on! Move away from here... I'm talkin' long distance...

(ELROI *moves away,* TEDDY *turns back to phone.*)

TEDDY: Yes ma'm. Put him on. Hello, Frank? What is goin' on? Unh-huh... unh-huh. We been waiting to go to the studio and...

ELROI: What's goin' on?

TEDDY: (*On phone*) Your sister? What about her?... so? Ain't you got sense, nigger? We supposed to be in Memphis at two o'clock. Elroi says the engineer is waitin' on us... He what?... When? If it was last night... Why didn't you call me, fool? We was supposd to be there, too...

ELROI: What about the session? What he say? They change it on us?

TEDDY: (*On phone*) I don't care 'bout that... I wanna know about our songs. SON OF A BITCH!

(TEDDY *slumps, letting the phone drop from his hand. The receiver bounces against the wall.* TEDDY *walks away from the phone, unable to talk. He stares vacantly out the window.* ELROI *is confused.*)

ELROI: What he say about our songs?

(TEDDY *doesn't answer.* ELROI *grabs the dangling receiver.*)

ELROI: Frank . . . Frank . . . you there? This is Elroi . . . Frank.

(*The line is dead.* ELROI *replaces the receiver, looks expectantly at* TEDDY.)

ELROI: What he say?

(TEDDY *remains turned away from* ELROI.)

TEDDY: Aint gonna be no recordin' session.

ELROI: How can that be? We had it all set up . . .

TEDDY: The engineer changed the time . . . it was last night . . . that's why he done left the hotel.

(*Turns to* ELROI.)

ELROI: Last night? How can the session be last night? He woulda called us . . . what about our songs? . . . we was supposed to be there, too . . .

TEDDY: Frank done his own songs . . . we been scratched offa the list.

ELROI: I don't believe it . . . Frank ain't like that . . .

TEDDY: (*Exploding*) WAKE UP, BOY! WE BEEN CUT!

(ELROI *stands frozen, shaking his head, unable to fathom the idea.*)

TEDDY: Our partner . . . Guitar Frank Jackson . . . the big man, you always talkin' up . . . done SOLD US OUT! (*Pause*) AND STOLE MY FORTY DOLLARS! To boot!

ELROI: No . . . can't be . . . no . . .

TEDDY: Yes, nigger . . . yes!

(TEDDY *tears at his own shirt, sweating profusely. He grabs the mojo, and rips the cord from around his neck.*)

TEDDY: Mojo hand . . . ignorant nigger voodoo! (*He hurls the mojo down.*)

TEDDY: Good luck, my ass! Give me the bad luck! Bring it on, Goddamn it, bring it on!

(TEDDY *and* ELROI *look at each other. Slowly,* ELROI *bends to pick up the mojo, holds it in his hand...* ELROI *looks at* TEDDY, *as the lights fade out.*)

End of Act One

Act Two

Scene 1

(*Time: A week later. Late evening.*)

(*Scene: The same.*)

(*AT RISE: Most of the lights in the barber shop have been turned off.* ELROI *is lying on the reclined barber chair, arm covering his face. He is listening to Johnny Ace playing quietly on the record player. The front door opens quietly.* FRANK JACKSON *steps into the shop, carrying a guitar case.* FRANK *is a tall black man in his early forties. He wears a new winter coat, a new cowboy hat, and a pair of new cowboy boots. He sets down the quitar case and closes the door quietly.* ELROI *does not hear him come in.* FRANK *takes off his gloves, blows on his hands, rubbing them together. He crosses to the heating grate and stands over the blowing heat.*)

FRANK: (*To himself*) Brr! Cold in Tennessee!

(ELROI *sits up suddenly.*)

ELROI: Frank?

FRANK: Who's there? That you, Teddy?

(ELROI *rises, turns on a light. He is still wearing the orange pants, but now with a different shirt.* FRANK *sees him and smiles broadly.*)

Well, I'll be . . . Orangebird, hisself. You glad to see me again, boy?

ELROI: (*Surprised*) Frank.

FRANK: Here I be . . . done blown across the river to see you special. And I brung somethin' for you. Bet you know what I'm talkin' about don't you?

ACT TWO

ELROI: Where the hell you been?

FRANK: Is that any kind of greetin' for your partner? Lighten up, Orangebird . . . I come back from down the Delta.

ELROI: You been gone over a week.

FRANK: I know that. Was you expectin' me for dinner or somethin'?

ELROI: Where you been?

FRANK: I been with my sister down in Helena . . . then I been in Memphis, and I played a few joints . . . both sides of the river, work my way north . . . and now I'm standin' here. What's with you? Where's Teddy? He in the back room?

ELROI: He ain't here right now.

(FRANK *hangs up his coat on the hooks, strolls into the back room, comes back out.*)

ELROI: What's the matter? Don't you believe me?

FRANK: Sure, boy . . . sure. So, where's Teddy?

(ELROI *shrugs.*)

FRANK: Out drinkin', huh? What you been up to?

ELROI: I should be askin' you that.

FRANK: (*Walks around the room.*) Makin' money, my man . . . earnin' my daily bread.

(FRANK *goes to the barber sink behind the chair, takes off his shirt, and fills the basin with hot water. He removes his cowboy hat and places it on* ELROI's *head.*)

FRANK: How you like that? Genuine Stetson. Got that hat in a Jew shop over on Beale Street. You like it? Looks real good on you. (*Indicates the mirror.*) Check yourself out. See? Pecos Pete . . . (*Laughs*) Orangebird on the range!

(ELROI *removes the hat, sets it aside,* FRANK *lathers his face with shaving cream. He finds one of Teddy's razors, begins stroking the razor on a strap on the chair.*)

FRANK: Five whole days now, I been dreamin' about a nice hot bath . . . and a good shave. Teddy ain't here . . . guess I have to shave myself. Where you say he is, Orangebird?

ELROI: I dunno . . . he went out after supper . . . maybe he gone for a walk.

FRANK: He say anything about me?

ELROI: Not much.

(FRANK *starts shaving. After a few strokes, he looks at* ELROI *in the mirror who is staring at him.*)

FRANK: You be awful quiet, Elroi. . . . You be thinkin' mighty hard on somethin', what might that be?

ELROI: I don't want you to call me Orangebird no more.

FRANK: (*After a pause*) All right, if that's what you want. I was only funnin' ya. . . . What you want me to call you?

ELROI: Nothin'.

FRANK: Nothin' it is, then. You wanna hand me that towel, over there?

(ELROI *gives him the towel.*)

FRANK: What's the matter with you? Ain't you never seen a man shave before? Somethin' buggin' you?

ELROI: You lucky you didn't come back here last Sunday night. Teddy was hot . . . he mighta killed you.

FRANK: Yeah, I know he wasn't too pleased . . . way things turned out. Not my fault . . . just happened, you know? My sister took sick . . . they done put her in the hospital. . . .

ACT TWO

ELROI: If I was you, I'd get out of here, 'fore he comes back.

FRANK: Oh? Teddy gonna start in a cuttin'... huh? (*Laughs*) I don't think so. He change his tune, when I show him what I got in that guitar case over there.

ELROI: I know what you got in there.

FRANK: What might that be?

ELROI: You know! Why'd you steal his money for a new guitar... then have to lie about it?

FRANK: New guitar? That what he told you? Shit! Ain't no new guitar...

(FRANK *opens the case, removes a red electric guitar, he plugs it into the amplifier... and tunes it.*)

FRANK: This here, ain't new... this is my "Emma-Jean", my ol' guitar. She done been locked up in the pawnshop for almost seven months... had to get her out. Never make a record without my Emma-Jean... kinda superstitious about things like that... she's my charm. You like her?

ELROI: If you got Teddy's forty dollars...

FRANK: I got it.

ELROI: Then leave it on the shelf... and you better get your butt back cross the river... he mad about that money...

FRANK: Forty dollars! That all he worried about? That ain't squat! How about I leave two hundred and forty there on the shelf. Maybe that make up for some of his troubles.

ELROI: You ain't got that kind of money.

(FRANK *reaches into his trouser pocket and removes a roll of bills. Places money on the shelf.*)

FRANK: Count it, boy.

(ELROI *counts the money,* FRANK *crosses to shoeshine chair, sits, and rolls a cigarette.*)

ELROI: (*Finished counting*) You rob a bank?

FRANK: Bet you ain't ever seen that much money in one place. That ain't even includin' your share, boy.

ELROI: My share?

FRANK: Yeah. Your wages . . . from them songs I recorded . . . "Can't Get Your Lovin' Off My Mind" . . . "Mean Disposition" . . . "Short-Haired Gal."

ELROI: You jivin' . . .

FRANK: No, I ain't.

(ELROI *whoops.*)

FRANK: See these boots? Brand new. (*Laughs*) Got kinda scuffed up in that Delta mud . . . maybe, you give me a quick shine job . . . I leave you a big tip.

(FRANK *laughs, picks up the guitar, strums a few chords.*)

ELROI: Tell me the truth, man. . . . Where did you get all this money?

FRANK: I done told you . . . makin' records, my man. That's what I do!

(FRANK *plays a fast blues run and begins singing,* "Can't Get Your Lovin' Off My Mind".)

I woke up with the blues on a Sunday
Had the same ol' thing on Monday
Now, Lordy, it's Tuesday already
I still ain't feelin' too fine
I think I smell me some trouble
It's got me seein' double
I just can't get your lovin' off my mind.

(FRANK *stops;* ELROI *jumps with excitement.*)

ELROI: You done it! You recorded my song!

Act Two

FRANK: What I been saying to you?

ELROI: You gone and done it . . . DAMN!

FRANK: I strolled right in there . . . pulled out ol' Emma-Jean, plugged her in, fired her up . . . and the man started ravin' about my sound. Just can't get enough of it. The man sends out for a bottle of Wild Turkey and some hushpuppies, and I set there over three hours, and I set down . . . oh, I don't know . . . must've been 17 or 18 numbers. . . . Man says he loves my sound. (*Laughs*) We rich now, Orangebird . . . I mean Elroi . . . we rich men. Pretty slick, huh?

(FRANK *plays a fancy guitar figure.*)

ELROI: Goddamn! I can't believe it! (*Pause*) But, you was supposed to take us along . . . that was part of the deal.

FRANK: Had to change it, boy. Man says he only got one microphone . . . and besides ain't much room in that recordin' booth . . . but, hell I brung ya the record . . . the first one they gonna release this week.

ELROI: They gave you the record? (*Looks in* FRANK'S *guitar case.*) Where is it? Lemme see . . .

(FRANK *closes the guitar case with his foot, holds it closed.*)

FRANK: Hold on . . . be plenty of time for that later. First, how about that shine I be needin'?

ELROI: I wanna hear our song.

FRANK: You get to it in a spell. How about you cleanin' the Mississippi offa these boots now? Maybe I give you an extra ten dollars, if you do a good job.

ELROI: You got a deal!

(ELROI *grins, grabs his shoeshine brushes, and goes to work furiously.* FRANK *lays a blues run while* ELROI *works.*)

FRANK: C'mon, boy . . . this is your song, sing it with me . . .

(*They sing together as* ELROI *works.*)

I woke up with the blues on a Sunday
Had the same ol' thing on Monday
Now, Lordy, it's Tuesday already
I still ain't feelin' too fine
I think I smell me some trouble
It's got me seein' double
I just can't get your lovin' off my mind.

Went to see my doctor just the other day,
Now I gotta tell ya what the man had to say,
He said, "You'll be feelin' funny
'Til you find that lovin' honey.
Got no pills to cure the achin',
my hands and feet are shakin',
Got these tears flowin' from my eyes,
My knees are feelin' weak.
Ever since you left me, baby,
I got a bad luck streak.

Can't nobody help me with this pain of mine?
Just can't seem to get her lovin' off my mind.

(*They laugh at end of song.*)

ELROI: So, tell me what happened. What the man say? What he say about the songs? He say he gonna show 'em to Elvis?

FRANK: Elvis? Hey, hold on. . . . All I done was cut some blues numbers. That's all. Weren't no Elvis Presley where I was . . .

ELROI: What did the engineer say? He like them songs?

FRANK: He loved 'em. The man said we might even get a hit record outta one of them songs.

ELROI: (*Whoops*) All right! Damn! You mean we gonna hear my song on the radio? Right here in Memphis?

Act Two

FRANK: Sure. You just wait, Elroi... it be on the radio before you know it.... Hell, folks all 'round the South gonna hear it.... They be singin' "Can't Get Your Lovin' Off My Mind" on their way to work every mornin'. It'll be on so many juke boxes... you'll get tired of hearin' it... be drifting outta every joint on Beale Street.... You'll see.

ELROI: Damn! We done it! I can't believe it. (*Pause*) You ain't just fuckin' with me are ya?

FRANK: No... I told ya... I recorded them songs.

ELROI: Man, what was it like?... I mean in the recordin' studio?... Did they make ya sign a contract?

FRANK: Contract! Shit, boy! I make 'em pay me cash. Never did trust them white boys' contracts. They pay me after each song.... I sing one, I gets the money ... then I do another one. They wants a third, they pay me right then... cash up front. Long as they keep the money comin' and the whiskey flowin' I play all night long. No white record company gonna cheat me again. I learned my lesson the last time I cut some sides, back in the forties. Always take the cash. I take a piss on their promises. See, you gotta let 'em know what's what.

ELROI: Right!

(FRANK *notices the cord under the collar of* ELROI's *shirt.*)

FRANK: What's that?

ELROI: What?

FRANK: That rope 'round your neck. What's that?

(FRANK *pulls it out.*)

FRANK: Well lookee here... got yourself a mojo. Where you get that?

ELROI: I found it.

FRANK: Conjure woman make that up for you?

ELROI: Yeah . . . she said it bring us luck. I was savin' it for you.

FRANK: Them things don't work. Few years back in Alabama, an ol' conjure woman give me a mojo . . . said it would turn my skin butterscotch brown. (*Looks at his skin*) Conjure woman was full of shit. (FRANK *plays and sings a quick ditty.*)

If you black, well get back,
If you brown, stick around,
If you white, well that's all right. . . .

(ELROI *finishes shining the boots.*)

ELROI: There . . . it's done.

FRANK: Mighty nice. Thank you, dad.

ELROI: Now, c'mon, I wanna hear that record. You promised . . .

(FRANK *steps down from the shoe shine chair. He takes a roll of money from his pocket, peels off a few bills, hands them to* ELROI.)

FRANK: I keep my promises, boy. Here's two hundred and ten dollars.

(ELROI *stares at the money, astounded.*)

FRANK: Well, ain't you gonna say somethin'? Or you gonna stand there with your mouth open? That there is more money than you ever made shinin' shoes. Go on, put it in your pocket.

ELROI: You mean, I get all this money?

FRANK: I told you. You earned it. For helpin' me out . . . you and Teddy . . . lettin' me store my gear in your place . . . feedin' me some meals . . . and . . .

ELROI: And them songs . . .

FRANK: And for that too. That's your cut.

ACT TWO

(TEDDY *comes in the front door, stops, looks warily at* FRANK.)

ELROI: Teddy, Frank . . .

FRANK: (*To* ELROI.) I got it, I got it . . . jes' be cool.

(ELROI *puts the cash in his pocket.* TEDDY *seems a bit tipsy.*)

TEDDY: Saw all these lights on . . . shoulda known you'd be back.

FRANK: Yeah. I come in tonight. Me and Elroi was just talkin' about you. He says you missed me. That true?

(TEDDY *ignores him. He hangs up his coat on the hook next to* FRANK'S. TEDDY *touches* FRANK'S *hat.*)

FRANK: That there's a new Stetson. You like it . . . I let you have it. Try it on.

TEDDY: Already got me a hat.

(TEDDY *removes a slab bottle of corn liquor from his hip pocket. He gets a glass from the shelf, and pours a drink.* TEDDY *notices the money lying on the shelf by the sink. He picks up the money, looks at* FRANK.)

FRANK: That's the forty dollars I borrowed . . . and some interest.

TEDDY: So, you done struck it rich, huh?

ELROI: Frank recorded them songs we wrote, Teddy. He says they gonna be on the radio this week. Teddy, we gonna be famous.

FRANK: Yeah. I come by to pick up my stuff . . . think I'll be movin' on soon . . . maybe go to Houston for a bit.

TEDDY: Good. When you leavin'? Tomorrow?

(FRANK *looks at* TEDDY *for a long moment.*)

FRANK: Okay . . . tomorrow.

FRANK: Hey, why I get the treatment from you? I come back and I brung you money . . . lots of it. I cut those songs we been workin' on . . . I thought you'd be happy about that.

TEDDY: I been listenin' to KWEM this week. I ain't heard it yet.

FRANK: Record just come out . . . in a coupla days maybe they play it . . .

ELROI: Frank brung the record, Teddy. I want to hear it.

(FRANK *opens his guitar case, takes out a 78 RPM record.*)

FRANK: Teddy, here 'tis. You want me to put it on?

TEDDY: Well it ain't gonna play itself, is it?

FRANK: (*To* ELROI) Nigger's jaws is tight.

(FRANK *goes to the record player, puts on the record.*)

FRANK: You gonna like this. Got a nice deep sound . . . bluesy like.

(*The song begins. A loping guitar figure.*)

ELROI: What the hell's that?

FRANK: That's the intro . . . just wait . . .

(FRANK'S *voice is heard singing. The song is a medium-tempo blues shuffle, much in the style of Lightnin' Hopkins or John Lee Hooker.*)

That's me . . . motherfucker! What you think? Sound good, huh?

TEDDY: Shut up . . . I'm listenin. . . .

ELROI: Man, it's too slow . . . too fuckin' slow. You got it on the right speed?

FRANK: Yeah, it's on seventy-eight.

Act Two

ELROI: Can't be . . . it's too slow . . . that ain't the right tempo . . . lemme see.

FRANK: (*Irritated*) Motherfucker, this is the way I recorded the song. I know if it's right.

TEDDY: Shut up.

ELROI: Man, it's all wrong! Teddy, it's wrong! That ain't the way it goes. It's supposed to be faster, like a jump tune.

FRANK: Jump tune . . . shit! It's the blues.

ELROI: Not even fast . . . shit nigger shuffle music.

FRANK: It ain't no rock-and-roll song! So just shut your face, 'fore I close it for you.

ELROI: You done it all wrong! Jive Ass! He done it all wrong!

TEDDY: (*Bellowing*) I'M TRYING TO HEAR THE FUCKING SONG!!!

ELROI: (*Kicks the wall*) It ain't like we rehearsed it!

FRANK: We rehearsed it? What did you do, boy? . . . Jes slap your hand on your knee while I played the guitar . . . that's all you did.

ELROI: You fucked it up!

FRANK: Who you be? You the expert on music? Jive ass, Orangebird!

(ELROI *is furious. He kicks* FRANK'S *guitar case.*)

ELROI: LYIN' MOTHERFUCKER! YOU RUINED MY SONG!

TEDDY: Elroi!

FRANK: Hey, don't you ever kick my guitar case! Boy . . . I'll cut your ass!

(FRANK *picks up* TEDDY'S *straight razor from the shelf.* TEDDY *tears the record from the turntable with a loud scratch sound.*)

TEDDY: That's enough! Put it down!!

FRANK: This dumb nigger done kicked my case.

TEDDY: MOTHERFUCKER! Put it down!

(FRANK *stands holding the open razor.* TEDDY *steps in to him, a stern warning*)

TEDDY: Don't make me get my pistol...

(TEDDY *stares* FRANK *down.* FRANK *lowers the razor, closes it and puts it back on the shelf.*)

TEDDY: Frank... don't you ever touch no razor in my shop!

FRANK: Then you tell this kid to keep away from my stuff.

(FRANK *goes over to examine his guitar case.*)

FRANK: (*To* ELROI) You just damn lucky that guitar wasn't in there. You hurt my Emma-Jean... you be dead meat.

ELROI: He was gonna cut me! You believe that?

TEDDY: Okay, okay. BE QUIET! Both of you!

(ELROI *takes the money from his pocket and throws it on the floor at* FRANK.)

ELROI: Don't want your money, nigger! You cheatin' liar...

(TEDDY *grabs* ELROI *and slams him against the wall, hand around his throat.*)

TEDDY: I SAID BE QUIET!

ELROI: Didn't you hear what he done to the song?

TEDDY: (*Choking* ELROI.) I SAID BE COOL! BE NO FIGHTIN' IN MY SHOP! YOU HEAR?

FRANK: Let the boy go, Teddy. You done choked off his wind.

ACT TWO

(TEDDY *releases* ELROI, *who coughs and spits into the sink.* TEDDY *gives* ELROI *a swig of corn liquor.*)

TEDDY: Here . . . drink this. You gonna be all right. C'mon, Elroi. . . . You sit down in my chair. I don't want to have to hurt you, but you out of control. . . .

(ELROI *sits in the barber chair, face in his hands.* FRANK *slowly picks up the money from the floor.*)

TEDDY: Now, the three of us gonna start actin' civilized. I ain't havin' the police come bustin' in here. (*Pause*) What's all that money on the floor?

FRANK: It's his. I give it to him for them songs. That's your split over there on the shelf.

TEDDY: Give it here.

(FRANK *gives him* ELROI's *money.* TEDDY *hands it to* ELROI.)

TEDDY: Go on, put it in your pocket.

(ELROI *hesitates.*)

TEDDY: Only a fool throw that much money on the floor.

ELROI: (*Pocketing the money.*) Still don't make it right.

FRANK: You's the strangest Orangebird I ever did see. Don't make no sense at all . . .

ELROI: That ain't my name. I'm Elroi . . . The King!

FRANK: King shit! That's what . . .

TEDDY: (*Warning*) Frank . . . lay off.

FRANK: Okay. I get my stuff, and I move on. That's what you want. You two done confuse me enough. Get me that record offa the victrola. . . . You wreck it?

(TEDDY *goes to the record player, looks at the record.*)

TEDDY: Got a big scratch across it . . .

(FRANK *begins packing up his things which are stored near the amplifier.*)

FRANK: Then you keep it...a souvenir of our association. I can get me another one somewheres else.

TEDDY: (*Reading the record label.*) "Can't Get Your Lovin' Off My Mind".

FRANK: "Mean Disposition" is on the other side.

TEDDY: Elroi, you wanna hear your song, "Mean Disposition?" I'll put it on if you wants.

ELROI: No, I don't wanna hear it...be the same crap as the other one....

(TEDDY *looks closer at the record label and frowns.*)

TEDDY: This ain't no Sun Records...What the hell is Jewel Tone Records?

(ELROI *looks up.*)

ELROI: Jewel Tone...where's that?

FRANK: They a blues record company outside Helena.

TEDDY: (*Reads label.*) I thought you gone to Sun...in Memphis...by Smilin' Frank...who's that?

FRANK: That's me...my new stage name...Smilin' Frank.

ELROI: Yeah, I just bet you was smilin' when you ruined my song.

TEDDY: Elroi, be quiet...Frank...how 'bout you explainin' this...Jewel Tone.

FRANK: I went down to Helena to see my sister. I cut them sides down there.

ELROI: You said you was goin' to Sun...said you had this engineer friend who was gonna fix it so we get to record in there.

FRANK: No . . . I said maybe that be the case . . . as it turns out, that engineer was just talkin' in his hat.

TEDDY: Then why you lie to us?

FRANK: I said maybe we gets in and maybe we don't . . . that's all I said! Now if you want to turn it all around . . .

TEDDY: That's not what we understood.

FRANK: Well you been understandin' only the parts you want to hear. That be a big problem with you, Teddy. You don't hear what folks says to you . . . you gotta read somethin' else into it.

ELROI: You said the engineer could get to Elvis.

FRANK: No, you said that! I only said, that he had seen Elvis in the studio. See what I mean? You two . . . like peas in a pod . . . know about as much as that ol' conjure woman, and she don't know shit!

ELROI: But you said the engineer could get 'em to Sam Phillips . . . they get us writin' songs for all them white cats. They record 'em and then they hit records . . .

FRANK: Whoa! Hold on . . . *I* recorded them songs. Anybody gonna have a hit record, motherfucker, it gonna be me! Not some ofay hillbilly with sideburns. It's my record, see! Where you get this pea-brained idea? (*Looks at* TEDDY) Need I ask! You been poisonin' this boy's mind, and that's a fact.

TEDDY: I wanna know why you had to sneak off to Helena . . . don't tell us one word 'bout what you doin' . . .

FRANK: You think back . . . you recall I told you last Sunday on the phone. But, do you listen? Hell, no! I done told you my sister took sick and they put her in the hospital . . . so, I grabbed a bus down there so there be someone to look after the kids while she's out. Now ain't that exactly what I said to you, Teddy?

TEDDY: I dunno . . . I don't remember.

FRANK: (*Mimicking* TEDDY) I dunno . . . I don't remember. (*Pause*) Damn good thing I ain't ever got any important messages for y'all.

TEDDY: I remember you said the time of the session was changed.

FRANK: It was. I went in Saturday night . . . instead of Sunday . . .

TEDDY: You talkin' about Jewel Tone! I'm talkin' about Sun . . . in Memphis! That's what we talkin' about! Don't weasel me . . . what about Sun Records? Let's get this straight. I know you said Sun . . . on the phone to me . . .

FRANK: (*Fed up*) Christ Almighty! All right . . . you wanna hear it? I give it to you . . . but you ain't gonna like it. (*Calmly roles a cigarette.*) I went over to Sun . . . to talk to the engineer . . . just to make sure it was all set for Sunday.

ELROI: When was that?

FRANK: I dunno . . . musta been last Thursday.

TEDDY: What happened?

FRANK: Engineer said no go! Somebody in the office got wind of it and the word come back . . . Sun Records ain't interested in recordin' colored singers no more . . .

ELROI: That ain't true . . . they got Howlin' Wolf . . . and Junior Parker.

FRANK: That was before . . . before this Presley kid got so big on them blues numbers he done stole from Big Boy Crudup. Engineer guy says they only recordin' these hillbilly cats now . . . this Carl Perkins, and a Johnny Cash. . . . said they don't need us no more. Said Sam Phillips been sayin' for years if he could just find him a white man who could sing like a colored . . . he could make a million dollars. Well, I guess he done found one.

ELROI: But those is colored songs they recordin'.

FRANK: So? When you see a white man pass up somethin' he wants for hisself?

TEDDY: (*Slow recognition*) You mean they ain't give no money to Big Boy Crudup for his song?

FRANK: Oh... you just figurin' that out? You learnin'!

ELROI: (*Looks at the record label*) Nobody done heard of Jewel Tone... Who's gonna play it?

FRANK: What do I care as long as they pays me.

ELROI: And why you let them call you somethin' stupid like Smilin' Frank?

FRANK: 'Cause it don't matter, boy. The last time I recorded they call me "Lonesome Frank"... time before that... "Blind Boy Jackson." White man can call me whatever suits his fancy... as long as he come up with the bread. Who the fuck you think runs this world, Orangebird?

ELROI: They done turned you into a joke!

FRANK: (*After a pause*) Yeah... so I be a joke to the white man. Don't mean I like it... but I do it... just like they wants. I stamp my foot to the music, I whoop and holler, flash a big ol' smile... I do what they says, 'cause they still runnin' this plantation, boy... and they pays my livin' expenses... you understand?

ELROI: You let 'em tell you how to sing 'em, too?

FRANK: (*Proud*) I plays the straight natural blues! I ain't no rock and roller! Not for nobody.

ELROI: Well, they ain't gonna turn me into no clown. Not me and Teddy.... Not our songs... they're gonna sing 'em the way we want, I'm gonna use my name... they gonna pay us royalties.

FRANK: Royalties? (*Laughs*) Royalty is for kings, Motherfucker! And contrary to what your Mammy done told you . . . you only the king of the shoeshine! And that's all you gonna be!

TEDDY: Frank . . . ease off!

FRANK: Who you think you are? The two of you . . . puttin' on airs . . . You some special type of niggers? (*Pause*) You done sold your shit . . . just like me . . . you no different.

TEDDY: What you mean?

FRANK: Them, songs, man . . .

ELROI: They our songs . . . we wrote 'em . . . we done the arrangements. . . .

FRANK: Whoa! Hold on! What's this we stuff? We done this . . . we done that. . . . I'm the man with the guitar . . . I'm the one on the record . . . not you! I made the deal with Jewel Tone . . . What did you do?

TEDDY: We done helped you write those songs.

FRANK: You helped on two songs. And I appreciate that, and you done been paid for your help. Thank you very much!

TEDDY: Three songs!

FRANK: How you get three?

TEDDY: "Short-Haired Gal". Did you record that one?

FRANK: Yeah . . . so?

TEDDY: I done give you the title. You was gonna call it, "Big-Legged Woman", but you done used my title instead.

FRANK: Oh, well, excuse me, Mr. Nalls, sir! You so right. I must owe you somethin'.

TEDDY: Damn right.

ACT TWO

(FRANK *peels off a fifty-dollar bill from his roll of money.*)

FRANK: How about fifty dollars? That take care of you for today? I thought so. Everything fine now.

TEDDY: Don't get smart with me.

FRANK: (*Holding out money.*) There's your fifty. Take it. I only gets a hundred for each song, so I figure fifty be worth more than the title. Don't you?

ELROI: How you figure a hundred for each song?

FRANK: 'Cause that's what the man pays me. I go in there with maybe twenty songs. . . . I record seventeen of 'em . . . and the man give me seventeen hundred dollars. I done give each of you two hundred . . . more than two hundred . . . seems more than fair to me

ELROI: You mean you sold my songs to the man? He owns them?

FRANK: That's right . . . he owns them.

TEDDY: Frank, you can't do that.

FRANK: Well, it's done. He do whatever he wants with them. They his now.

(ELROI *lunges at* FRANK, *knocking him off his feet.* TEDDY *struggles to pull* ELROI *off* FRANK.)

ELROI: You can't sell my songs . . . they mine . . . I'm gonna kill you.

TEDDY: Hey . . . c'mon . . . Elroi . . . stop it . . .

FRANK: Get that crazy fool offa me!

(TEDDY *holds* ELROI's *arms, but he struggles violently.* FRANK *gets up, grabs* ELROI, *and speaks directly in his face.*)

FRANK: Hey! Hey . . . you listen to me, Boy. I done you a favor. Did I ask you to write songs for me? Did I ask you? No. I had my own songs . . . but here you come . . . stickin' 'em in my face . . . "Here, sing this . . . how about this?". . . . So, I did. Just like you wanted, Elroi. I done right by you. And now you been paid for your work! What more you want, nigger?

(TEDDY *glares at* FRANK. *He releases* ELROI. ELROI *collapses to the floor, howling and moaning.*)

TEDDY: Frank . . . you done gone too far!

FRANK: Time this boy growed up . . . see things for what they is. And that goes for you, too!

(ELROI *rolls around on the floor, crying. He curls himself into a ball.* FRANK *walks away in disgust, crosses to the shelf and takes a long swig from* TEDDY'S *pint of corn liquor.* TEDDY *kneels next to* ELROI, *trying to comfort him.*)

TEDDY: Elroi . . . listen to me. It's gonna be all right. We write some new songs . . . you and me . . . we write 'em together . . . what you think? Come on, . . . get up off the floor.

(TEDDY *helps* ELROI *to his feet* . . . ELROI *stands for a moment staring with hatred at* FRANK. FRANK *does not respond.* ELROI *spits at the floor by* FRANK'S *feet.*)

ELROI: LIAR!

(ELROI *turns and runs out the front door of the shop.* TEDDY *goes to the door calling after him.*)

TEDDY: ELROI . . . don't run off . . . Come on back here . . . Elroi . . . ELROI!

FRANK: You be wakin' up the whole neighborhood.

TEDDY: He run out in the cold without his jacket.

(TEDDY *goes to the hooks and puts on his own coat and scarf.*)

FRANK: Jes . . . let him be.

TEDDY: I gotta go find him.

FRANK: He be long gone by now . . . you'll be lookin' all night. He come back when he gets cold. Just his pride . . . that's all that hurts.

(TEDDY *stands for a moment by the open door, looking at the street. Finally, he closes the door, turns to* FRANK *who is standing by the sink, drinking the corn liquor.*)

TEDDY: You sholdn't have done that.

FRANK: He get over it.

TEDDY: He just a kid.

FRANK: (*Pause*) You been soft on him ever since his Mama died.

TEDDY: I said I'd look after him. (*Pause*) No reason for it. . . . What you done to that boy tonight . . . there ain't no excusin'.

FRANK: Time some folks learned they ain't hangin' the moon for us out there.

TEDDY: We know that, but there's nothing wrong with him hoping and you done spit in his face.

FRANK: No . . . I done showed him how it is.

(TEDDY *looks at* FRANK *for a long moment, then turns, and goes out the front door to find* ELROI. FRANK *shakes his head, and drinks from the pint of corn liquor. The lights fade out.*)

Scene 2

(*TIME: That same night, almost four in the morning.*)

(*SETTING: The same.*)

(*AT RISE: A single light over the sink is the only illumination in the shop.* FRANK *is seated in the barber chair, alone with his red electric guitar, which is plugged into the amp nearby.* FRANK *is wearing trousers, his boots, and undershirt, and his new cowboy hat. The empty pint bottle is on the floor by the chair.* FRANK *is quietly strumming and improvising bluesy runs on the guitar.* FRANK *reaches down for the bottle. After draining the last drops from the pint, he tosses the bottle across the room toward the record alcove.* FRANK *broods. He plays another blues run, and breaks into a boogie-woogie rhythm. He taps his foot to the beat, and starts singing in a deep, menacing voice.*)

FRANK: (*Singing*)

I'm goin' to Louisiana
Gonna get me a Mojo Hand
I'm goin' to Louisiana
Gonna get me a Mojo Hand
I'm gonna fix my woman
So she can't love no other man.

(*Instrumental break*)

I'm layin' down thinkin'
'Bout that Mojo Hand
I'm layin' down thinkin'
'Bout that Mojo Hand
I'm gonna fix my woman
so she can't love no other man.

(FRANK *plays a bridge to the song as the phone rings.* FRANK *stops playing, looks at the phone. He sets the guitar side, turns off the amp. He ambles to the phone, and answers.*)

FRANK: Teddy's Barber Shop.... Hey, Teddy... where are you! It's almost four in the morning. You see Orangebird, yet? No, he ain't called here. Why don't you come on back ... be sunrise in an hour or so ... he'll come home when he's good and ready. You just wastin' you time ... the streets is empty, everybody sleepin' ...

ACT TWO

(FRANK *notices something outside the window. Headlights and the sound of a pick-up truck outside.*)

FRANK: Hold on a minute . . .

(FRANK *looks out the window, goes back to the phone.*)

FRANK: You know anybody with a red pick-up truck . . . Mississippi plates? Naw, me neither . . . well, one just pulled up outside. Can't tell who . . . I dunno. Where you keep that pistol of yours? Well, you better get your butt back here. They gettin' outta the truck now . . . two people . . . comin' this way . . . I gott go now.

(FRANK *hangs up the phone, and stands to one side where he will not be seen. He looks at the figures outside the window. As they approach the front door,* FRANK *slips quietly into the back room. The front door opens and two people stumble into the dimly lit shop. It is* ELROI *and a white woman,* MAXINE PETTIBONE. *She is holding him up.* ELROI *is very drunk and he sings incoherently. They stumble toward the barber chair. She struggles to get him to the barber chair.* ELROI'S *face has many cuts and bruises. His shirt and trousers are soiled and torn.* MAXINE *is a somewhat pale and plain girl in her late twenties. She wears a dress and cloth coat, carries a purse.* MAXINE *speaks with the unmistakeable accent of poor people from the Delta area.*)

MAXINE: This is it. We made it. (*Calls out.*) Anybody here? Come on, into this chair . . . just a few more feet. Up you go. That's it.

(*She maneuvers him into the barber chair, tries to find the lever to tilt it back.*)

There . . . now where the hell is the control lever on this thing? Here it is. . . .

(*The chair reclines half way.* FRANK *watches from the curtain area.*)

MAXINE: (*Calling out, again.*) Anybody here? (*To* ELROI) You sure this is the right place? There's nobody here. Maybe this ain't the right barber shop.

(ELROI *mumbles.*)

MAXINE: What you sayin'?

ELROI: Get Teddy. . . .

MAXINE: Who is Teddy? I don't know no Teddy. You want a teddy bear? Is that what you want?

(FRANK *steps into the room. He turns on the light switch.* MAXINE *turns quickly, scared.*)

MAXINE: Oh, Jesus, save me! You scared me half to death. . . .

(FRANK *moves toward her and* ELROI.)

MAXINE: Who are you? You Teddy?

FRANK: No, I'm Frank.

MAXINE: I . . . I brung him home . . . he got in some trouble.

FRANK: What happened to his face?

MAXINE: He got in a fight with some white boys.

FRANK: Friends of yours?

MAXINE: No . . . God, no . . . we were mindin' our own business . . . I swear . . . and these boys come and start sayin' stuff . . . I brung him in my truck. He asked me to take him home. I didn't know what else to do.

FRANK: This boy smells like a still.

MAXINE: He drank himself a whole pint of corn liquor.

ELROI: (*Singing*) She got a mean disposition . . . meanst gal' I ever seen . . .

MAXINE: Shh. You gotta settle down now, Elroi.

ACT TWO 57

(FRANK *gets a bottle of peroxide from the shelf.*)

FRANK: I'll take care of him.

(MAXINE *steps aside as* FRANK *tends to* ELROI.)

FRANK: Now shut up, boy. Quit your singin'. Now this is gonna sting a bit . . . but it'll be okay . . .

ELROI: Ow! . . .

FRANK: Now hold still, Elroi. I'm tryin' to fix you up.

MAXINE: Elroi told me he was a singer. Said he used to sing in a group with Johnny Ace. You know Johnny Ace?

FRANK: Yes, ma'am. He dead now. Shot hisself.

MAXINE: I know. I cried when I heard that on the radio. I was listenin' to WDIA that night. . . . They was playin' "Pledgin' My Love", and Jimmy Mattis, he come on the air after the song, and all he could say was, " . . . Johnny's gone . . . Johnny's gone . . ." Kept sayin' it over and over . . . he started cryin', right there on the radio.

FRANK: (*To* ELROI) You're gonna have a hell of a head in the mornin'.

MAXINE: (*To* ELROI) You're gonna be all right. You just had too much to drink, that's all. (*Lullabyes* ELROI.)

"Forever my darlin'
Our love will be true. . . ."

(*Again to* ELROI) Shhh. . . .

(MAXINE *notices the posters of Johnny Ace on the wall.*)

MAXINE: Wow! You got his picture, and his record album on the wall. God, he was really somethin' . . . I seen that show! That one right there! God, was it great! I drove all the way up here . . . wanted to stay for both shows, but, I couldn't . . . besides . . . second show was only for the coloreds, you know? (MAXINE *discovers the record bin*) Damn! Look at all these records. Golly, look at this stuff—Joe Turner, Ray Charles. You can't buy these records for love nor money down where I live. Folks down there . . . they hate this kind of music. "Coon jump", that's what they call it. What do they know? Ain't ever heard nothin' but Roy Acuff and the Grand Old Opry— bunch of stupid yodellin' peckerwoods—if you ask me. Hey, how much you want for that B.B. King picture?

FRANK: Not for sale.

MAXINE: Oh. (*Pause*) Tell me somethin' . . . was Elroi just talkin', you know, when he said he sung with Johnny Ace? He just make that up?

FRANK: Elroi ain't no singer. He's a songwriter.

MAXINE: I see. You're the singer, ain't ya?

FRANK: That's right.

MAXINE: I figured. You look like a singer. (*She starts to pick up* FRANK'S *guitar.*) I bet this is your guitar. Real purty . . .

(FRANK *takes the guitar from* MAXINE *and puts it away in the case.*)

MAXINE: Would I know any of your songs?

FRANK: No, Ma'am.

MAXINE: So tell me . . . where the hell am I?

FRANK: I think you on the wrong side of town. This is West Memphis.

MAXINE: Arkansas?

FRANK: Yes, ma'm. West Memphis, Arkansas. You ain't from around here.

MAXINE: No. I come from Mississippi . . . Senatobia. You know where that is?

ACT TWO

FRANK: Yes, ma'm, I do . . . north end of the Delta.

MAXINE: That's right.

FRANK: You work down there?

MAXINE: Me? Work? (*Laughs*) No . . . my husband does . . . he's a salesman . . . farm machinery. We got ourselves a little place down there. Sometimes on the weekends . . . I . . . uh . . .

FRANK: You drive up to Memphis . . . have a little fun . . .

MAXINE: Yeah, somethin' like that . . . (*Pause*) Tonight I come up to see Guitar Slim. He's got that hit record out now, "The Things That I Used To Do." You know that song? I love that song. He's playin' at the Pearl Lounge this week. . . . Did you know that? (FRANK *shakes his head, "no"*.) Heard all about it on Rufus Thomas' radio show. You know, "Hoot and Holler?" I listen to it every night. . . . Well, nights when, Earl . . . that's my husband . . . nights he ain't in the house. He can't stand all that colored music, you know?

FRANK: Where be this husband of yours? He out in the truck?

MAXINE: In the truck? No . . . he's down in Jackson, 'til tomorrow . . . on business. So . . . I come up to Memphis. I like to hear them singers in the juke joints. (*Pause*) Nothin' wrong with that. . . .

FRANK: No, ma'am.

MAXINE: I just love them rhythm and blues songs. Makes you wanna get up and dance. Sometimes a person's just gotta let loose . . . have a good time . . . right?

FRANK: Yes, ma'am.

MAXINE: Don't say that: "ma'am. I hate that. Nigras back home say that all the time. Why don't you call me . . . Maxine. That's my name . . . Maxine Pettibone.

Some of my friends call me, "Maxie"... I don't mind...

(FRANK *regards her for a long moment.*)

MAXINE: Why you lookin' at me so funny-like?

FRANK: I don't think I'll be callin' you nothin'.

MAXINE: What do you mean by that?

FRANK: I knowed a white woman like you before... was nothin' but trouble.

MAXINE: What are you insinuatin'?

(*Front door opens* TEDDY *enters. He stops when he sees* MAXINE.)

TEDDY: What the hell is goin' on here? (*Pause*) Who's she?

FRANK: This is Mrs. Maxine Pettibone, from Senatobia, Mississippi.

MAXINE: Hi!

TEDDY: What's she doin' in my shop?

MAXINE: I brought Elroi home. Are you his father? Are you a singer too?

(TEDDY *moves to the barber chair, and examines* ELROI.)

TEDDY: Elroi. What happened to him? Who did this?

FRANK: Got drunk and got his ass beat.

TEDDY: (*To* MAXINE) You responsible for this?

MAXINE: (*Follows* TEDDY.) No... I was tryin' to help him.

TEDDY: Elroi... you hear me? How you feel?

FRANK: I put some peroxide on them cuts... he'll be all right.

TEDDY: Elroi... talk to me, boy....

ACT TWO   61

MAXINE: I think he done passed out.

FRANK: He was dead drunk when she brought him in here.

TEDDY: You get him drunk?

MAXINE: No, I did not.

TEDDY: Suppose you tell me exactly what you done.

MAXINE: I was drivin' in Memphis . . . when I seen him hitchhiking on the road . . . lookin' all cold and pitiful . . . so, I gave him a ride . . . just like any decent Christian woman would do . . .

FRANK: Then they went to some gin mill.

MAXINE: That ain't what happened! Were you there? No, you weren't. He bought the corn liquor himself.

TEDDY: But, you done drunk it with him.

MAXINE: I don't like what you're suggestin' . . . not one bit!

TEDDY: Just tell me what happened after you picked him up . . . on the road.

MAXINE: Well . . . he got into the truck . . . and then I asked him where he was goin' . . . and he asked me if I could take him to some recordin' studio . . . over near the Memphis 'Lectric Company. . . .

FRANK: Sun Records.

MAXINE: That's the one . . .

TEDDY: In the middle of the night? Why'd you go over there?

MAXINE: I dunno . . . I tried to tell him . . . I thought they'd be closed, but he kept insistin' that he knew somebody in there . . . and they was gonna let him in . . . so he could sing his song . . . or somethin' . . .

FRANK: Fool idea . . .

MAXINE: So, we pull up . . . and all the windows are dark, but he gets out and starts bangin' on the door. He was makin' a terrible racket . . . I just knew the police was gonna come by any minute . . . so, I went out on the sidewalk . . . and I was tryin' to get him back in the truck 'fore somebody come to see what all the hollerin' is about . . . and then these boys came down the street.

TEDDY: White or colored?

MAXINE: White . . . 'bout five of 'em . . . and they been drinkin' too . . . and they seen me tryin' to pull him into the pick-up truck and they started sayin' things . . . you know. And then, Elroi . . . he sees 'em and he gets it in his head that one of these fool boys is Elvis Presley. . . . Now I knew it wasn't Elvis, 'cause I seen pictures of him. You know? Well, Elroi started talkin' back, smart like . . . and they got to pushin' and shovin' . . . suddenly, they were all on top of him . . . I started yellin', and they took off . . . I put him in the truck and I brung him over here. . . .

TEDDY: Why didn't you take him over to the hospital . . . get them cuts tended to?

MAXINE: I don't know where the colored hospital is. I ain't from Memphis.

(TEDDY *starts for the pay phone.*)

MAXINE: Hey, what are you doin'?

TEDDY: I'm gonna call the police.

MAXINE: No . . . You can't do that. I mean . . . they see me here . . . what are they gonna think?

TEDDY: What do I care what they think?

MAXINE: Now, look, my husband would kill me iffin' he knew I was here. You can't get me involved.

TEDDY: You already involved . . . you done got him drunk . . . got his ass kicked.

ACT TWO 63

MAXINE: I already told you . . . that ain't my fault! Now, I brung him here . . . that's all I'm gonna do.

TEDDY: Oh, no. You gonna tell the police what you know about them boys. They ain't gettin' away with this.

FRANK: Teddy . . . careful . . .

MAXINE: Now, I'm warnin' you . . . you call the police, and I'll tell 'em that three niggers kidnapped me. . . . brung me across the river to rape me. You'll get yourself in a lot of trouble. You understand?

TEDDY: Woman, I'm done foolin' with you!

(TEDDY *drops the phone, starts toward* MAXINE.)

MAXINE: You stay away from me. Don't you dare touch me. Don't you ever try to touch me, boy!

(TEDDY *lunges for* MAXINE. FRANK *jumps between them, grabs* TEDDY *and pushes him away from her.*)

FRANK: NO! Teddy . . . NO! You can't do this! Now, stop! The lady's right, Teddy. There be trouble for us all. Besides . . . you call 'em, what they gonna do when they hear some colored boy done got his ass beat by some hillbillies? They laugh . . . that's what they do.

(FRANK *settles* TEDDY *into a chair.* TEDDY *is breathing heavily.* FRANK *turns to* MAXINE.)

FRANK: Lady, you better get the hell home 'fore your husband finds out what you been up to.

MAXINE: (*Moves toward the door.*) I done nothing wrong with this boy!

TEDDY: Go on . . . get outta my shop! There be plenty of farm bucks down there in the Delta to occupy your time . . . don't have to drive all the way up to Memphis . . .

MAXINE: (*Moving toward door.*) I'm sorry as hell about what happened to this boy, but it ain't my fault. I just come up here to hear some music. ... that's all.

(MAXINE *exits.* TEDDY *slams the door.*)

TEDDY: Music, my ass!

(FRANK *looks at* TEDDY *for a long moment. Sound of truck engine starting up outside.*)

FRANK: Is you crazy, nigger? Where's your sense? All that woman has to do is tell the police. . . .

TEDDY: I don't care what she says.

FRANK: Yeah, well, you'd sing a different tune with a rope around your neck. Now, you better cool off, Teddy. . . . You playin' with the Devil. . . . What the fuck is wrong with you?

(TEDDY *doesn't answer. He puts a cold, wet compress on* ELROI's *face.* TEDDY *puts on his coat and scarf.*)

FRANK: Where you think you're goin'?

TEDDY: I'm goin' after them white boys.

FRANK: Oh, and how you gonna find 'em? They be long gone, now.

TEDDY: I'll find 'em. . . .

FRANK: You plannin' to walk to Memphis in the middle of the night?

TEDDY: If I have to. Done walked farther in boot camp.

(TEDDY *finds his pistol in a box on one of the shelves. He puts the pistol in his coat pocket. He turns.* FRANK *stands in front of the door, blocking his way.*)

TEDDY: Now, get outta my way, Frank. I know what I'm doin'.

FRANK: I ain't lettin' you walk outta here. You crazy, Teddy. Now, calm down, man.

TEDDY: Stand aside, Frank.

ACT TWO

FRANK: No, Teddy. I ain't gonna let you get yourself shot by no cracker over in Memphis. You wanna kill somebody? Then kill me. Kill me, goddammit! I ain't movin'.

TEDDY: I'm mad, Frank! I'm mad.

FRANK: I know it ... but you can't do this.... You know it, Teddy. You can't. This ain't London. ... Ain't never gonna be like it was back then.

(*Tears well up in* TEDDY'S *eyes. He throws a 78 RPM record against the wall in frustration.* TEDDY *howls in anguish. He thrashes wildly about the shop. He rakes the items off a shelf.*)

TEDDY: Goddamn them! Goddamn it ...

(TEDDY *smashes one of the records on the floor.*)

TEDDY: Lyin' cheatin' motherfuckers!

(TEDDY *hurls a record at the wall with the picture of Johnny Ace.*)

TEDDY: Fuckin' Johnny Ace!

(TEDDY *is winded by his outburst.* TEDDY *gasps for air, holding his chest.* TEDDY *sits heavily on the shoe shine stand, trying to control his breathing.* FRANK *goes to the sink, fills a glass with water.* FRANK *brings the water and* TEDDY'S *blood pressure medicine to* TEDDY.)

FRANK: Easy, Teddy ... easy now, man ... take your medicine.

(TEDDY *takes the pills, washes them down with water.* TEDDY *takes off his coat, fans himself with a newspaper.*)

FRANK: You want me to get you a doctor?

TEDDY: No, I'll be okay in a minute. Just let me sit a spell.

(*They are silent for a long moment.*)

FRANK: I know how you feel, Teddy.

TEDDY: Do you?

FRANK: Yeah.

TEDDY: (*Gestures to* ELROI.) I can't let nobody shame this boy . . . nobody.

FRANK: Well, this boy mighta got some of them starry ideas knocked outta him tonight, but Elroi gotta take his lumps just like the rest of us.

TEDDY: Oh, yeah . . . you's a fine one to talk. You ain't the one that's been here with him every day. I'm the one that buys him a new pair of shoes. I'm the one that makes sure he gets somethin' to eat . . . I'm the one who's gotta put him back together tomorrow.

FRANK: I see. You be thinkin' maybe somebody owes you somethin' . . . I see how it is.

TEDDY: Nobody owes me nothin'.

FRANK: That a fact?

TEDDY: I only want what's best for him.

FRANK: No, I think maybe you wants a little bit for yourself, too . . .

TEDDY: What the hell you mean by that?

FRANK: Elroi ain't the one, Teddy. It's you, I'm talkin' about . . . You been kickin' my butt 'bout lettin' the boy down . . . steppin' on his hopes . . . but, you been wantin' that hit record more than him.

TEDDY: You's full of shit!

FRANK: That may be! But there was a time when you wanted more than this barber shop. Back in the old days when we was runnin' around Beale Street . . . we'd see Louis Jordan at the Palace, or you'd catch my act at Dinky's . . . I watched you listenin' to the music, all the time knowin' that you wished it was you up there on the bandstand.

ACT TWO 67

(*Long pause*)

TEDDY: And, if I could've played the guitar as good as I cut hair, I'd've put you outta business.

FRANK: I believe that. But what would it've gotten ya'? . . . a beat up old suitcase full of dirty clothes . . . an old guitar . . . that needs a new set of strings.

TEDDY: And your pockets full of money!

FRANK: Shit, the money's nothin', Teddy. It be gone in a month or two . . . then I be three steps ahead of the revenue man . . . money just slips through my fingers like rainwater. I don't even know where it goes . . . some juke joints along the river . . . a woman over in Hot Springs . . . some whore down in Mobile . . . I ain't in one place long enough for the dust to settle.

TEDDY: Why you live like that?

FRANK: So I can make music . . . that's what I do. The cards have been dealt, Teddy . . . you cut hair . . I play music.

(TEDDY *looks at* ELROI.)

TEDDY: What about this boy? He ain't gonna grow up shinin' shoes forever . . . and I sure as hell don't want him takin' over this shop after I'm gone. What's he gonna do?

FRANK: First thing he gonna do . . . is get over the hangover he's gonna have.

TEDDY: (*Chuckles*) Yeah, his ass gonna be sore in the mornin'.

(*They laugh.*)

TEDDY: Tell me straight, Frank . . . his songs . . . are they good enough to get on the radio? Are they?

FRANK: I went into Jewel Tone . . . I recorded seventeen songs . . . and outta them seventeen . . . the only two they pressed into records was "Mean Disposition" and

"Can't Get Your Lovin' Off My Mind". You figure it out.

TEDDY: The boy's got talent.

FRANK: Yes, indeed.

(TEDDY *rises, goes to barber chair.*)

(TEDDY *looks at* ELROI *for a moment.*)

TEDDY: I'll tell you one thing, Frank. . . . I'm gonna make sure he gets his chance. He's gonna do it. I'll see to it, he does . . .

FRANK: Yeah, I bet you will.

TEDDY: We oughta get him outta this chair. Come on, help me lift him up. We'll put him on the bed in the back room. . . . Let him sleep it off.

FRANK: You get the top, I'll get these ol' orange legs.

(FRANK *and* TEDDY *lift* ELROI *from the barber's chair.* FRANK *sings,* "Can't Get Your Lovin' Off My Mind"— *at the slow bluesy tempo.*)

FRANK:

Well, I woke up with the blues on Sunday
I had the same ol' thing on Monday . . . Now, Lawd
   it's Tuesday . . .

TEDDY: Frank. If you're gonna sing the boy's song, then you sing it the way he wrote it.

FRANK: You got it.

(FRANK *sings the up tempo version, and* TEDDY *joins in as they carry* ELROI *toward the back room.*)

BOTH:

Woke up with the blues on Sunday
I had the same ol' thing on Monday
Now, Lawd, it's Tuesday. I still ain't feelin' so fine
I think I smell me some trouble
It's got me seein' double
I just can't get your lovin' off my mind.

(*Lights fade as* FRANK *and* TEDDY *continue to sing the song.*)

End of Play

CAN'T GET YOUR LOVIN' OFF MY MIND

Lyrics by Martin Jones

Music by Rick Snyder

Med. Blues

CHORUS
dou - ble. I just Can't Get Your Lov-in' Off - a My
E7
E7
sim.
Mind No — I just Can't Get Your
E7
E7
E7
VS. 2
Lov-in' Off - a my Mind I
E7
E7
went to see the doc-tor just the o-ther day Now I got to tell you what the good man
N.C. (E7)
had to say, He say, (spoken) "Hey man... You don't look so good"... But there's
(A7)

no-thin' I can do for you. Ya see, you'll be feel-in' real
fun-ny 'Til ya find that lov-in' hon-ey. I just
A7 A7
CHORUS
E7
Can't Get Your Lov-in' Off-a My Mind
E7 E7
sim.
No — I just Can't Get Your Lov-in' Off-a My Mind
E7 E7 E7
Vs. 3
POSSIBLE INSERT INSTRUMENTAL
I got no pills to cure this ach-
E7
N.C. (E7)

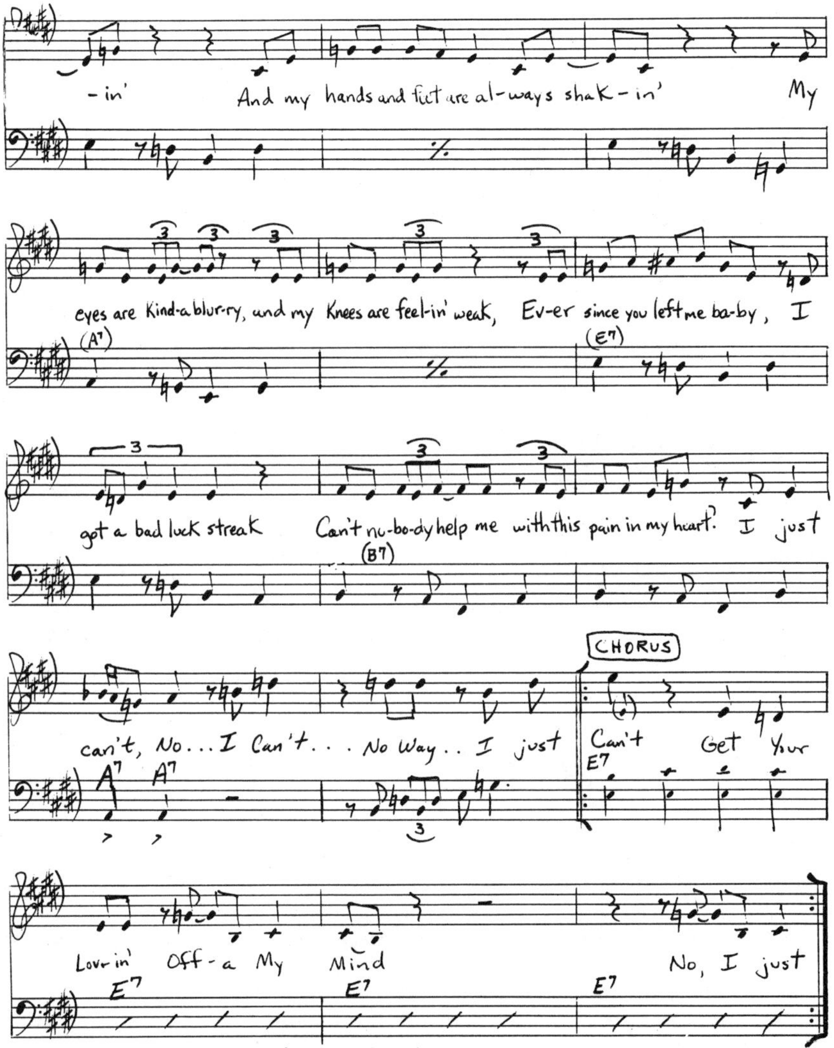

VAMP AD. LIB. to END AD. LIB.

MOLLY BAILEY'S TRAVELING FAMILY CIRCUS

featuring

SCENES FROM THE LIFE OF MOTHER JONES

BY MEGAN TERRY & JOANN METCALF

A musical presentation of magical and possible events in the lives of **two women** born in the last century. The Omaha Magic Theater (where **Megan Terry** is the playwright in residence) has toured this show around the Mid West. A minimum of three males and four females, though it can be expanded to accommodate a greater number; may be done with simple fluid staging.

NATIVE SPEECH

BY ERIC OVERMYER

A riveting play, rich in texture and rife with allusion, which provides a chilling vision of civilization about to go belly up. Originally produced at the **Los Angeles Theater Center** in the summer of 1983. Seven males, three females, though one more of each can be used. Single interior set plus an exterior playing area.

BATTERY

By Daniel Therriault

Electricity is the central metaphor and expressive image in this unusual love story which takes place in an electrical repair and systems design shop located in Chicago. Therriault has an exceptional ear for American speech patterns, and has been **compared to Sam Shepard and David Mamet for his superb use of language.** First produced in New York at St. Clement's Theater in the Spring of 1981. Two males, one female; single interior set.

SAGA

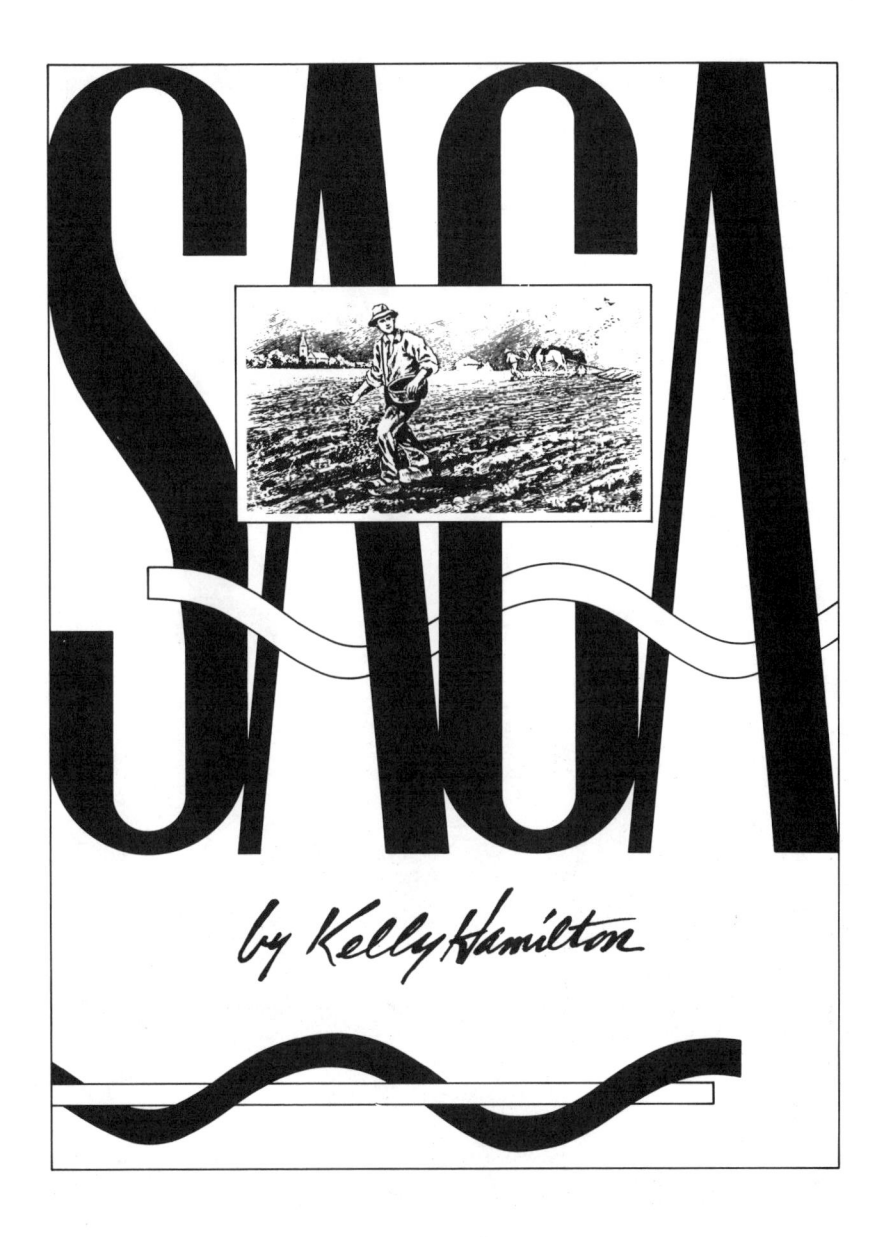

by Kelly Hamilton

This wonderful **musical** is a history of America's pioneers as they push their way across the country. A minimum of eight males and eight females are necessary, and the show can be expanded to use many more actors. Settings can be fluid and simple or elaborate.

This delightful small scale **musical** is about the life of **Gilbert and Sullivan**. It is interspersed with some of the best known songs from the Savoy operas, including THE PIRATES OF PENZANCE, HMS PINAFORE and THE MIKADO. This show had a very successful run on the West End of London in 1975, and subsequently at the **Actors Theater of Louisville**. Five males, three females, though more actors may be used as "stage-hands" and chorus members.